*B*UT I WANT to know more about your people, how they love and make love."

Her creamy white bosom rose and fell a little more quickly as she asked this daring question. Her eyes, lit by the camp-fire, could not or would not find his in the evening darkness.

"You might not like what you find," he finally answered, his voice as hard as his body. "It is a privilege we reserve for a select few. Are you strong enough for such a journey?"

The flames danced off his naked torso as he fed more wood onto the fire. Part of her was afraid of the passion this aboriginal man aroused in her, but another part craved what he could teach her.

But she was no child. She was a woman. And he was a man. Her voice quavered as she answered.

"Teach me."

And he did.

AN EXPLORATION

OF NATIVE SEX

AND SEXUALITY

Me

Compiled & Edited by
Drew Hayden Taylor

Sexy

Douglas & McIntyre

VANCOUVER/TORONTO/BERKELEY

08 09 10 11 12   5 4 3 2 1

Douglas & McIntyre Ltd.
2323 Quebec Street, Suite 201
Vancouver, British Columbia
Canada v5T 4S7
www.douglas-mcintyre.com

Library and Archives Canada Cataloguing in Publication
Me sexy : an exploration of native sex and sexuality /
compiled and edited by Drew Hayden Taylor.

ISBN 978-1-55365-276-2

1. Native peoples—Sexual behavior—Canada—Humor. 2. Native peoples—
Sexual behavior—Canada. 3. Native peoples—Canada—Humor.
4. Canadian wit and humor (English) I. Taylor, Drew Hayden, 1962–
E78.C2M457 2008   306.7089'97071   C2008-900000-5

Editing by Scott Steedman and Iva Cheung
Copy editing by Iva Cheung
Cover and interior design by Peter Cocking
Cover illustration by Ryan Heshka
Printed and bound in Canada by Friesens
Printed on acid-free paper that is forest friendly
(100% post-consumer recycled paper) and
has been processed chlorine free.
Distributed in the U.S. by Publishers Group West

We gratefully acknowledge the financial support of the Canada
Council for the Arts, the British Columbia Arts Council, the Province
of British Columbia through the Book Publishing Tax Credit,
and the Government of Canada through the Book Publishing Industry
Development Program (BPIDP) for our publishing activities.

CONTENTS

INTRODUCTION

*W*HEN I TOLD people I was thinking about putting together a book about the world of Native sexuality, the two comments I got back most often were: (1) "That will be a short book" and (2) "Isn't that a contradiction in terms?" Usually these comments were said with a knowing smile, but I knew there was a grain of social belief buried deep within. And I thought, "If only they knew . . ."

Welcome to what could be called a textbook about some of the most private issues in Native culture. It has been said that how a people makes love or expresses love says more about who they are than all their political, social and economic writings. Once, when I was at a powwow, a vice-chief from the Assembly of First Nations approached me. He had read some of my essays and found them less than serious or effective. "Have you ever thought about writing about something important, like self-government?" he said.

At that time, in a precursor to this book, I had been working on an essay detailing the dominant culture's perception of Native sexuality. So, at this powwow, I went around and asked ten people which they would be more interested in reading or thought was more relevant to their lives: an essay on self-government or an essay on Native sexuality. I don't think I have to tell you which answer I got.

In 2006 I compiled and edited a book exploring and deconstructing the world of Aboriginal humour. It was called *Me Funny*. My original reason for tackling that subject was a wish to educate the dominant culture about the many varied and colourful (no pun intended) aspects of Aboriginal life. Society and its media machines have often painted us as being stoic, tragic, alcoholic and basically oppressed, depressed and suppressed. To a lesser extent, a lot of our own literature has done the same thing. If you believed what you read, we were a sad, sad people.

But experience had taught me that this was not the case, and other people across Canada needed to know it. So I decided that part of my journey in life would be to show the public how wonderfully developed, highly refined and downright hilarious our sense of humour really is. Thus the book *Me Funny*, which got an excellent response. The word was getting out.

After it came out, though, I started thinking—a potentially dangerous activity for an unemployed writer. I started to wonder what other misinformation or erroneous beliefs existed out there regarding the Aboriginal peoples of this country. Then it came to me. Romance. Passion. Sex. Erotica. Playing the snake-and-hollow-log game. All that fun stuff. Since that fabled age known as Time Immemorial, we, the First Nations people of this country, have all been *intimately* familiar with our delightful practices of passion, but for reasons unknown, members of the dominant culture have other perceptions about said topics. They have a different frame of reference. For instance, they think of the Latin lover, the French lover, the Italian lover, and so on. You never hear about the studly Salish lover or witness sly knowing glances when mentioning the Naskapi lover or shudder at breathless sighs brought on by the thought of an Ojibway lover. What a travesty, and not just for the Salish, the Naskapi and the Ojibway. The general public did not know what it was missing.

Most often, Canadians hear about Native sexuality in their media in a more negative context. Sexual abuse in residential schools. Native hookers being killed. AIDS rates reaching epidemic proportions in many First Nations communities. Et cetera. Although many of these stories are unfortunately true, they are only a minuscule portion of the stories out there that reflect the vast ocean of Aboriginal sexuality. There needed to be some re-education. Someone needed to float a boat on that ocean. And on a more personal note, I felt a book on the topic could quite probably be just as much fun as, if not more fun than, *Me Funny*. Thus was born *Me Sexy*.

Start paddling.

Within these pages you will read about topics as varied as erotic Inuit theatre, how sensual and sexy the Cree language can be, what our art has to say about how we bump uglies and where we fit in amid today's complex sexual society. It's a potpourri of information in thirteen interesting essays. Think of it as a "How to make love to a First Nations person without sexually appropriating them" type of book. It will inform you. It will shock you. It may make you laugh. It may even make you blush.

But above all else, this is a book about honesty, love and survival—three qualities that make for an excellent date.

Me Sexy.
You Sexy.

DREW HAYDEN TAYLOR

BUSH COUNTRY

Joseph Boyden

ONE TIME, MANY years ago, while living in Moosonee, Ontario's last, great outpost before it's all bush planes and freighter canoes to get farther north, I ended up at a house party near the ambulance station. The party wasn't well attended, which was no fault of the host, a genial white guy who'd lived in Moosonee for many years and seemed to truly care for the town and its people, the majority of whom are Cree. He'd gone much further than most of the transient white population in making friends with the locals of both Moosonee and the nearby reserve of Moose Factory, and, as far as I know, he still lives there today.

He was a good guy, from what I remember, but he had a few redneck friends at this party who were not. One of them in particular I will never forget. He was a big, scary-looking guy, clad in the northern tuxedo of lumber jacket and jeans, clearly very strong, and just drunk enough to want to go at it with anyone in the house he figured he could beat up. If memory serves, he was one of those guys Ontario Hydro hired from some small town in northern Ontario or Quebec to clear bush from Moosonee straight north to Fort Albany and Kashechewan in advance of the hydro poles that would eventually connect those isolated reserves to the rest of us.

He was the kind of white guy even other drunk white guys of his build and bravado didn't want to mess with. He'd just come out of the bush after a long mid-winter stint and clearly needed, but wasn't going to get, sexual release with one of the few women at the party. He stunk of frustration and paced around the house for a while, saying hello to the women. But as soon as they stopped talking to him, which didn't take long, he grew frustrated. And, as I sensed would happen from the moment I saw him, he decided to focus his pent-up frustrations on me, a long-hair at the time. He made it clear he didn't like me. Not in that "Outside now so I can beat your ass dead" kind of way—he hadn't drunk enough yet. Instead he tried to get me to make the first move so that he could pound me and then tell our genial host, "The ponytail threw the first punch! I was just protecting myself."

He began his conquest of me in the kitchen—where else? I sat at the table with our host's girlfriend, whom I'll call Claire, a pretty Cree student of mine. The redneck, let's call him Dale, took a beer from the fridge and, seeing us talking and having a good time, zeroed in and proceeded to twist the beer cap in his sausage fingers into something that looked like a DNA strand, then demanded that I try this party trick, too. I'm a writer, for Christ's sake, I wanted to tell him. But instead I tried to play along, twisting off the cap of a new one. The hiss of the carbonation, when I think of it now, was foreshadowing. I took a large gulp of the beer to show him I was a party guy too, put the bottle down, picked up the cap between thumb and fingers and began trying to twist. Not a chance in hell. Failure hurts. "Ouch," I said for emphasis when the sharp edge cut into my finger. Dale smelled blood. I think he thought that his show of strength might win over Claire. He decided to go in for the kill.

"You got hair like a girl," he said, looking at me. Claire giggled, so he kept going. "Are you a girl?"

I nodded coyly. Amazingly, my spur-of-the-moment strategy worked; he didn't know how to respond. I have three brothers and seven sisters, all of whom have beat me up at different times, so I wasn't too worried about fighting if I had to. I had Claire as backup, to boot.

Not drunk enough to go right then and there, Dale decided to engage in a little verbal jousting. I think he realized the night was still young, and if he were to get kicked out of a house party in Moosonee this early, his options would be sorely limited. Ontario Hydro bunkhouse. The same well-worn and weary copy of *Penthouse*. Or worse, the OPP drunk tank.

"What is someone like *you* doing in Moosonee?" Dale asked. Good question.

"I'm a teacher," I said. Round one to Dale.

"A teacher? You?"

"Those who can't twist beer caps, teach," I said. Round two? A draw. Confusion in his eyes, Dale turned his attention to Claire, licking his lips. "Are you his girlfriend?"

Claire giggled. "Ever!" she said, drawing the last syllable out.

"You're too pretty for him," Dale said.

"Ever!" I responded.

Our genial host re-entered the kitchen. "Come on, you guys. Let's be friends," he said, sensing the tension.

Dale pounded his beer and grabbed another from the fridge, making a show of twisting the cap once again. "Do you know what I like about Indian girls?" he asked, looking Claire in the eye. "They barely got any hair on their pussies. Just a little black fuzz. Almost like a kid."

The three of us just stared, puzzled at the non sequitur. The gross, icky non sequitur. Dale's words shut me down. Round three decisively to Dale. Claire's face reddened. She stood up and walked away. Our host followed. I looked at Dale. He smiled. "I love Indian pussy," he reiterated, "because it's almost hairless."

How do you respond to that? I didn't know. Still don't. A whole race and gender objectified, and the whole thing somehow tied in to pedophilia.

I remembered that moment for a long time. I think because I didn't stand up and defend my friend. Or Aboriginal women. Or any woman. I just sat there at that kitchen table, a long-hair chicken sipping a beer.

I'll admit I had a few daydreams not long after that night about standing up and confronting Dale, making him understand. But understand what? His words were the basest of confrontation. When you want to offend a man, you attack the woman. If the man doesn't stand up, he's a pussy. An almost hairless pussy, in my case? Dale won, I guess.

Not. Dale is a pig. Dale is probably dead or in jail. Or worse, and hopefully, he's still out there, his hairy ass being chewed off by mosquitoes or frozen ice-white by the James Bay winter as he futilely attempts to clear bush, so to speak, in Indian country.

And so the years went by.

My old friend of Mexican and Apache heritage—I'll call him Matt—and I were drinking beers on my porch, complaining to one another about the slow recovery of our Katrina-ravaged city, New Orleans. The wrongness of what happened to this city, how all of my local Houma Indian friends had been washed away by the flood. About wrongness in general. We drank some more, starting to one-up each other about what was wrong.

"You want to hear something that's wrong?" Matt asked.

"Tell me," I said, opening another beer.

"It's really wrong," he warned. It all started back when Matt and his friend were twelve or so, during those sad, pubescent years. Once in a while, Matt would shower at his friend's house, and vice versa. Don't ask me why. I never got around to the question. Maybe both friends' families had pools, or the boys slept over at each other's places every so often. I'd like to think of this part of the story, anyway, as innocent. But the story begins one day when Matt's friend showered after Matt and was grossed out that Matt had accidentally left a few pubic hairs on the bar of soap. And then the next time they showered one after the other, Matt commented that his buddy had done the same. Maybe at first the two were both intrigued and mortified by the strange powers of their maturing bodies. And, as only pubescent and then post-pubescent boys can do, these two friends created a grotesque tradition.

Whenever the opportunity arose that one would shower in the same place right after the other, the first made sure that a number of strands of curly dark hairs remained on the soap for the second to see. I can understand this sort of prank in high school, maybe even college. But it continued, as only men can continue such a tradition. Now the two friends, living in different cities with girlfriends and respectable jobs and bills to pay, only got to visit each other occasionally. But their ritual persisted.

Who knows who upped the stakes? But, as Matt relates it, one time, during his buddy's visit, Matt found a couple of foreign pubic hairs on his toilet seat lid and one or two on the sink. They certainly weren't Matt's girlfriend's. He knew her well enough. And so when Matt next visited his friend, he did something that made him giggle and gag at the same time. Matt plucked more than a few of his short and curlies and carefully placed them into his friend's shampoo bottle.

That, in my opinion, is only asking for trouble.

Matt's friend's retaliation? Think carefully camouflaging a few pubic hairs into the bristles of Matt's toothbrush. The gag of foreign itchies sticking to the back of his throat. There's not enough Listerine in the world for that experience. So wrong, this thing we call retaliation.

Now, I don't want you thinking that I think about pubic hair very often. Truth is, I rarely do. But Matt's and my recent conversation re-invited that jerk from so long ago back into my head. This in turn made me wonder, if only for a brief time, if, by chance, Dale somehow knew something I don't. That night, I asked Matt about Dale's theory. He scratched his thinly bearded chin. "Only one way to find out." He suggested we compare our pubic mounds.

"We're both mixed bloods, though," I said. "What would that prove?"

Matt shrugged. He was drunk. I explained to him that the two of us were too tainted as subjects for such an important scientific experiment—Matt by his genes from the conquistador Spaniard, me with drunken Irish and cheap, cheap Scottish. For a moment, though, I imagined my gene pool, hairy little Irish and Scottish genes attacking my proud but rather sparsely haired Ojibway genes, the Ojibway genes snared in finely woven traps. I realized at that moment that I'd had one or two beers too many out on my porch.

But over the next few days the question continued (in a small way, admittedly) to gnaw at me, until I finally decided to put my rather minor and renewed fascination with a bizarre comment made long ago to rest. Do Aboriginal women (and men, for that matter) have sparser pubic hair than other races?

Immediately, the difficulties presented themselves. First and most important, I'm married to a gorgeous but non-Aboriginal woman, Amanda. She's of German descent, and, as it happens, she's almost hairless in the nether regions. So desperately trying to get Indian ladies to show me their womanly bits wasn't going to fly. I considered the Internet as a source for my research, but a few excursions into the cyberworld yielded either sociological examinations of race, with nary a pubic hair in sight, or some really dirty pictures of women who didn't look Native at all giving their best for the camera. And it took a lot of explaining and reassurance on my part to explain to my wife that this online sleuthing wasn't simply an excuse to look at porn. I even encouraged Amanda to sit beside me when I began googling. She passed.

Another idea sprung up, if only momentarily. What about placing an ad in a couple of carefully chosen classified sections? "If you are an Aboriginal woman or man with pubic hair, please contact me for a short but clinical discussion." I'd read stranger ads in the back of *now Magazine* in Toronto and the *Georgia Straight* in Vancouver. I'd even recently met the young and energized Sarah Scout, editor for an Aboriginal youth magazine in Calgary called *New Tribe*. She might cut me a deal on a classified ad! But wait—was there a slim chance that people might not understand my true intellectual intentions and try to brand me as some kind of pervert for pursuing this research? The potential trouble outweighed my slight thirst for knowledge.

Frustrated and defeated after a couple of days, I decided to scrap the whole project. How ridiculous to even approach it. What would complete strangers think of me, this guy, proposing such a stupid hypothesis? What if my mother were to one day get her hands on this essay?

To my surprise, it was Amanda who urged me not to give up. She reminded me that it wasn't the hair so much as Dale's racism and sexism so long ago that had driven me to explore this issue in the first place. She was right. "Why don't you call a few of your Native buddies up north and ask them if they think it's true?" she asked.

I immediately pictured myself calling Louise Erdrich, one of the great Aboriginal writers of our time, in Minnesota to pose the question. "Louise, I know you are mixed blood, but in your experience, do you think you have less pubic hair than women of other races?" Or I could call the handsome and imposing Thomas King in Ontario. "Now Tom, I assume you have at some point in your life had to shower with other men—men of different races, even. Did you notice anything peculiar? I know you wouldn't purposely look at other men's private parts in the shower, but when you did, did the white guys appear hairier down there?"

Not the best idea, dear wife.

But I had a few other options. I have a Moose Cree friend way up in northern Ontario who is one of the great hunters and trappers of James Bay. My friend, let's call him William, lives in Moosonee, and we have been close for many years. We've spent weeks in the bush together and have shared a lot, although I don't ever recall us seeing each other naked. Who better to ask? I came up with all kinds of excuses to put off the call. There was laundry to do. Dirty dishes. A new novel to write. But when I couldn't stall any longer, I picked up the phone.

"William, it's Joseph." How to approach this? Be direct! I imagined starting the conversation: "William, does your wife—let's call her Pam—does she have a lot of pubic hair, or a little pubic hair, or somewhere in between?" Silence on the other end. "William? Are you there? I'm only asking for purely scientific reasons."

Instead, we began our conversation as we always do, telling each other about the weather in our particular territories, me asking him when he was going out into the bush next. The bush. I found my entrance into my real reason for calling.

"I'm, uh, I'm writing an article about pubic hair. Specifically, whether Native people have more or less pubic hair than other races."

"Joe, I haven't been with another woman for twenty years. I can't remember."

Hmmm. "What about Pam?" William and I go way back. This would be a test of how far.

"I'm married, Joe. I try not to look down there." Ahh, William. He's a trickster. His wife is beautiful. They had a new child not so long ago.

"Liar."

"Well, less than most other people, I guess. I think it's because Indians are more highly developed than other races." Hard to disagree with that.

"But wouldn't it make more sense for a people like the Cree," I asked, "a people who live in such cold climates, to have lots of body hair to keep them warm?"

"That's what rabbit fur's for, JoJo."

I heard Pam shouting at the kids on the other end. "Ask Pam," I said.

Garbled talking. A laugh. "She says the Indian women she's seen naked are pretty bushy sometimes. Sometimes not. Are we talking full blood, mixed blood?"

"Just generally, William."

"Well, my grandma, she was full blood and didn't have any hair under her arms. Does that count?"

"I guess. What about you? Are you furry down there?"

"Compared with a rabbit, no. I don't really have any way to compare."

I asked William if he wouldn't mind doing an informal poll for me of some of his friends. It took some work, but he actually did it. Unfortunately, not a lot came back. A few of the women claimed they couldn't wear bikinis. Lucky they live in the Arctic lowlands. Many shared that they had little or no armpit hair. None of the men William polled had much of anything to say on the matter. When it came down to the bottom line, I didn't learn much I didn't know already.

But do I really need to? Before getting off the phone, Will and I made plans for a spring fishing trip, an annual occasion where I bring my son and William brings his family and we spend a number of days on the river fishing and laughing and cooking shore lunches. Some of the best memories I have.

I could go on about how people like Dale will always attempt to denigrate me and my friends and Indian women and women in general. I could go on about how he tried but failed, and I could talk about how in the spring I'll be up fishing with my friends, and we'll talk and we'll laugh and we'll let our pubic hair down, so to speak, and enjoy one another's company. How we might even compare bushes or maybe even decide to pluck part of our pubic hair out and place it in a communal bucket, and when we have enough we'll weave gillnets for pike and sturgeon, braid strong snares for rabbit and fox. I could go on about how we'll all be there together, me and my friends, continuing to entwine our mutual hair into long beautiful braids, braids that go on and on. But I won't.

Is there some lesson to be learned from this? I'm skeptical, except for the fact that I shouldn't ever have let some ass get me so worked up. Mohawked or Brazilian, gloriously full or bald as an eagle, who, ultimately, really gives a damn? The beauty of the bush is in the eye of the beholder.

PRE-CHRISTIAN
INUIT SEXUALITY

Makka Kleist

There was a little ptarmigan
sitting on the lowland
on top of a snowdrift
red were its eyelids
brown down the bag
and in between its small behind
was a dearest little bottom

A POEM FROM WEST GREENLAND,
ORIGIN UNKNOWN

INUIT, AS A PEOPLE, were probably the only nation that didn't have any intoxicants at all. My ancestors didn't have alcohol or herbs that they could use as drugs. The only "high" they could get was from fermented food, which was eaten only at very special occasions.

So, after a good meal—most likely of fermented food—they would turn off their lamps. They would sit in total darkness and either await someone to grab them or go hunting for a partner themselves.

When the sounds of utmost physical pleasures had died out, the lamps were lit again. Then they would spend the rest of the evening telling stories, singing—the body full of a good meal and exciting sex!

Our forefathers were very aware of the dangers of degeneration, being so few people and living in very small settlements. Mixing blood was vital to our survival.

In our pre-Christian culture sexuality was considered a necessity to the body, as much as food and water, and hence we didn't have so many taboos or hidden agendas regarding sex. However, since we were so few people we had a strict rule against incest. Degeneration could wipe out the whole nation, so new blood was always welcomed.

Our myth about how the sun and the moon came to be goes as follows:

Once there was a family with two lovely children, a son and a daughter. When the children grew into adulthood, they were allowed to participate in the "turn-off-the-lamp" games.

The young girl, being very attractive, was always "touched" immediately after the lamps got dark. She enjoyed her partners immensely every time. After some time she started noticing that it was the same man who sought her out. She got very curious. Next time it got dark she smeared her hands with soot and marked him. When the lamps were lit again, she discovered to her horror that her brother's skin was full of soot. She took a knife, cut off one of her breasts, dipped it in the lamp oil and lit it. With her breast as a torch she ran out of the house. She had such a force in her movements that she levitated and became the sun.

Her brother grabbed a stick, lit it and ran after her. He too started flying, becoming the moon. But his torch wasn't as strong as his sister's, so it almost died out. He blew on the stick, and sparks flew out and became the stars.

So to this day Aningaaq, the moon, flies after his sister, Seqineq, the sun. Sometimes they are very close to each other, but Seqineq always manages to keep her distance from Aningaaq, and she always has a much brighter glow, whereas he always has to fight for his.

In all Inuit cultures, from Siberia to Greenland, the sun is female and the moon is male. Very few other cultures on our globe have that combination. The moon, Aningaaq, controls ebb and flow and has an influence on fertility, menstruation and abortion. The sun, Seqineq, is the life-giving, warm nurturer.

Until recently the husbands would stow away the softest part of the hare skin. Since the man had an influence on his wife's menstruation he would take his responsibility for it and give his mate the softest skin to wear as a sanitary napkin every day during her "moon."

NO GENDER HAD an inherited dominance in matters of sexuality—both could take the initiative, and both could enjoy themselves. Sex was not only considered a physical necessity equal to water and food, but it was also regarded as a tool to help one's emotional well-being. Sex was not just connected to our genitals or just an act of procreation; it was a necessity to our sanity.

Foreplay and cuddling were as important as the actual act itself.

When a hunter came to one's village—maybe after days or weeks of hunting alone in the wilderness—it was a must that he should be fed, given water and, when going to bed, offered the place next to the wife. They need not have sexual intercourse, but if that happened it was never a big deal; in fact, it was expected. The most important part of the experience was, however, to give the guest the possibility to cuddle and feel the warmth of another human body.

In the mask dance—one of our oldest theatrical traditions— sexuality is pivotal. But functions of the dance are different for the children than for the adults.

On a quiet evening—preferably in wintertime—a strange being would suddenly enter the room. Its face would be totally unrecognizable. It would have a tied-up nose, a stick in the mouth, a face covered with soot in intricate patterns, a body distorted either with an enormous penis if the actor is a female or, if the actor is a man, with larger-than-life breasts (forget Dolly Parton!). The stick, by the way, is said to represent the balls.

First of all he or she has to be funny. The clowning around was an important part of the ritual.

Second, the being must be scary, and *that* is for the children. It is very important that children learn how to handle fear. Fear is a very strong psychological emotion that could cost you your life if you don't know how to react to it. Many of the children will at some point later in their lives experience being totally alone, and if they panic or don't react at all, they could either damage their souls for the rest of their lives or even die. We can't afford to lose any souls, with so few around. The idea is that if you can handle fear then you can handle most of the other strong emotions that you will encounter in your life. You learn that emotions will come and go and that you can deal with them. Don't freeze, but react! Seeing the reactions of the adults—they scream, run, laugh or start to interact with the actor—shows the children that it is okay to show your feelings.

The most important part for the adults is the being's sexuality. The actor makes fun of the parts of the body that focus on physical sex and acts out movements to the point of being vulgar—a sexual encounter is just a physical act.

Even after Christianity did its utmost to distort sexuality for us, we still don't have the word "promiscuity" in our language. We have a translated word, of course, but it doesn't have its origin in our Greenlandic Inuit language.

A TRADITIONAL DWELLING in wintertime had a whalebone or a wooden frame and was made of turf. It had a narrow, tubelike entrance, a room used also for storage, and then a very high door sill leading to the living space "upstairs," since the coldness will always seek the lowest point. On one of the longest walls would be a long plank bed, a bed for everybody—everybody being the whole household of father, mother, children, grandparents, uncle, aunt, cousins . . .

The children heard or saw what went on between the adults during the night. The children not only saw that sex was a natural part of life, but they also learned how to do it.

They became great lovers!

> He came with the warm
> winds of the south
> came to me like an
> animal never seen before
>
> making sounds so pleasantly
> I didn't even notice
> he was beginning to crawl
> inside of me
>
> smell of unnamed spices
> and earth shaking of a hunger
> for even deeper sounds
>
> juices running down from my breast
> to the North pole—the big navel
> Qalasersuaq
> melting the ice
>
> and then
> the dam bursting
> bursting
>
> and then . . . uhm . . .
> the taste of the saltiest raw
> oyster I ever ate

INDIAN LOVE CALL

(minus Jeanette MacDonald
and Nelson Eddy)

Drew Hayden Taylor

A shameless girl approached me with affrontery,
offering to keep me company, for which I thanked
her, sending her away with gentle remonstrances,
and I passed the night with some savages.

SAMUEL DE CHAMPLAIN[1]

THE DOMINANT CULTURE'S skewed perception of Native sexuality dates back many centuries, perhaps to the very point of contact. And the results were usually unpleasant. In the early 1500s, Hernando Cortes had an Aztec interpreter and mistress named Malinche who, according to history, was instrumental in the downfall of Aztec civilization. Ever since, Mexicans have smeared her for her traitorous acts by giving her the unpleasant nickname "La Chingada," which loosely translates as "the Fucked One." The term is still a common insult in Mexico today. It was not an auspicious beginning.

In her essay "Sexuality and the Invasion of America: 1492–1806," Vicki Jaimez says that, "For Europeans, sexual allurement manifested itself in the forms of sex as reward (officially incurred or not) for service to country, sexual interaction as politics or sport, and fascination with Native displays of European taboos. In addition, they were led by a desire for sex for the sake of pleasure, as a form of comfort in a land far from home."[2]

Western literature teems with such representations, which say a lot more than their authors intended; literature is the DNA that tells the truth about the culture that bore it. Many, for instance, have argued that Caliban in Shakespeare's *The Tempest* is a Eurocentric fantasy of indigenous lust and depravity, the man who put the *id* in idiopathy. Ariel, another indigenous resident of the island, was a spirit and thus physically and motivationally out of reach (but still fully controlled by Prospero), but Caliban was an indigenous creature of flesh and blood and not a very nice person with not very nice interests:

PROSPERO: Thou most lying slave,
  Whom stripes may move, not kindness! I have used thee
  (Filth as thou art) with humane care, and lodged thee
  In mine own cell till thou didst seek to violate
  The honour of my child.
CALIBAN: Oh ho, o ho! Wouldn't that have been done!
  Thou didst prevent me; I had peopled else
  This isle with Calibans!
MIRANDA: Abhorred slave! . . .[3]

Even more revealing, Caliban was the son of the island's resident witch (a symbol of the indigenous culture's spiritual leader?), whom Prospero supplanted upon his arrival, forcing Caliban to serve as his slave. Manifest Destiny delivered in iambic pentameter.

In the succeeding centuries, many books told tales of sexual relations between Native and non-Natives, and, as can be expected, the courtship was difficult. My personal favourite is Injun Joe in Mark Twain's *The Adventures of Tom Sawyer*. This half-breed speaks fondly of many depravities, from grave robbing to theft to one particular form of pleasure. Speaking to a fellow outlaw, he confides what he has in mind for a local white woman:

> When you want to get revenge on a woman you don't kill her—bosh! You go for her looks. You slit her nostrils—you notch her ears like a sow's![4]

John Seelye, a Twain academic, writes, "Having been horse-whipped by her late husband, Joe plans on tying the widow to her bed and mutilating her, an episode linked by Dixon Wecter to an incident in which an actual rape (not by an Indian) may have been threatened—a theme hardly suited, as Wecter notes, to a children's book. Yet, to an adult reader, the image of a woman tied to a bed is hardly subliminal, and the episode has its literary counterparts in [Last of the] *Mohicans*, where the evil Huron named Magua seeks revenge against Colonel Munro, who has had him horsewhipped for drunkenness, by kidnapping Munro's daughter Cora and attempting to force her into marrying him, a 'cruel fate' with a clearly sexual dimension. But Injun Joe is much more than a social menace: he is evil personified, doing bad things because he likes to."[5]

And, of course, he ends up starving to death trapped in a cave, outwitted by a precocious young white boy. Karmic retribution.

Over the intervening years, little has changed. There might be fewer face mutilations and less overt racism, but manifestations of Aboriginal sexuality in literature still have less fact and more fiction than they ever have. The Internet and other new media have merely opened up the possibilities for further exploitation and misinformation. The medium isn't the message anymore. It's the problem.

In the vast majority of non-Native literature, Aboriginal char-
acters, just as they never have a sense of humour, are rarely ever
viewed as sexual beings. And if they are, their sexuality is not
healthy. What we did and how we did it is dark (no pun intended),
foreboding and forbidden. Kidnappings, rape and other assorted
defilements are the order of the day on this particular pop culture
menu. Tender love stories involving Native people are scarcer
than priests at a residential school reunion. We never even had a
Romeo and Juliet story. Granted, it's a tragic, dysfunctional tale
(about families, ending in multiple suicides), but we'd even accept
that. Over the years, there have been many rumours and legends
about the true relationship between Tonto and the Lone Ranger,
but that's about all we've got (and that's a whole different essay).

Speaking of cowboys and Indians, in John Ford's classic
movie *The Searchers* John Wayne spends five years looking for
his niece, played by Natalie Wood, who has been kidnapped by
Comanches. When he finally finds her, rather then letting her
live peaceably and amicably with her Native husband and his
people, he intends to shoot her to save her from such a dishonour-
able existence. Sort of an early American honour killing. Instead,
he finds redemption by destroying the village, scalping the chief
and returning the girl to her white family.

Earlier in the movie, Wayne, as Ethan Edwards, is watching a
white woman and her two daughters who have been recently rescued from Indian captivity. In the screenplay they are described
as "mad," "frightened," "wild-eyed" and as making "animal
noises." They are bordering on insanity.

COWBOY: It's hard to believe they're white.
ETHAN: They ain't white. Not anymore. They're Comanch'.

In an essay on Ford, Joan Dagle says this scene "clearly con-
veys not only the absolute opposition between Indian and white

settler, but also the underlying fear and threat of sexual violation and attendant madness."[6]

From now on, I will remind myself to be nicer to the white women I date.

It has only been within the last fifty years, since the era of political correctness began, that the concept of exploring Native sexuality has become possible, if not downright interesting and, in some cases, quite fashionable. In the age of the New Western, it's hard not to bring two films and their contemporary views of Native sexuality into the conversation: *Soldier Blue* (1970) and *Dances with Wolves* (1990).

In *Soldier Blue* (with a theme song by Buffy Sainte-Marie, so you know it's authentic), Peter Strauss plays a cavalry officer who "rescues" Candice Bergen, who has been kidnapped by Native people years before. The other soldiers, less in touch with their feminine side, openly gossip about how many bucks she's been with. But Bergen's character is portrayed as being much more savvy and logical than her rescuers; in the new era, turnabout is fair trade. And the cavalry officer is no longer seen as the rescuing hero—he is now less honourable than his traditional enemy. If the cavalry comes riding over the hill to rescue you from the Indians, hide and seek refuge with the Indians.

This concept is pushed even further in *Dances with Wolves*, often to a ridiculous extent. The white woman is the only person in the Indian village in desperate need of a comb, and the soldiers sent to civilize the American Plains are a ragtag bunch of mercenaries, bullies and buffoons. For a change, the European conquerors are not portrayed in the best of light. There is no one except Kevin Costner—who at first seems so ill-equipped, both materially and mentally, to survive in this rugged landscape—to be the conscience of his people.

But perhaps the most telling part of the film was the tame sex scene in the teepee. Costner wakes up and sees Graham Greene and Tantoo Cardinal going at it. And lo and behold, Tantoo is on top. For years afterwards I would hear women, sociologists, film students and a host of other people with too much time on their hands commenting on and approving of the fact that they had shown the woman on top. "What a progressive statement," they would say. "It showed how respected the woman was in traditional Native culture"—and various other similar opinions.

Ironically, in porn terminology that position is called "cowgirl," not "Indian girl." I sometimes think that, as a stand against Manifest Destiny, as a statement objecting to cultural genocide and Christian indoctrination, to further limit the encroachment of the dominant society's thunderous existence and virus-like contamination, First Nations people around the world should ban the "missionary position," in light of the bad historical baggage it carries. Or rechristen it the "Aboriginal position."

HOW TIMES HAVE changed. And how they haven't.

In 1983 the fledgling medium of video games crossed a new frontier when the company Mystique marketed a new game it had developed for its Atari 2600 series. It was called *Custer's Revenge*. The marketing copy went as follows:

> History was never quite like this. In a "creative interpretation" of the Battle of Little Big Horn, a rowdy and naked General Custer must make his way through a hail of continual arrows to a Native American princess tied to a pole. If Custer can survive the obstacles in his way, he then gets an opportunity to have "sexual intercourse" for big points. Whether his needs have been sated, or brought down by enemy fire, Custer will return again and again to get what he wants.[7]

Class question: How many things are wrong with that sales pitch? And if you answer that traditionally, Native Americans never had a hierarchy of royalty, so the term "princess" is inaccurate ... well, then maybe somewhere out there is a cultural sensitivity course with your name on it. And did I say "the era of political correctness" earlier? I take that back.

I remember seeing a news report about the launch of this game and the public outcry, especially from women's groups and Native organizations, that predictably followed. It told me two things: computer games are designed by adolescent boys and their adolescent imaginations, and the battle continues. I also seem to remember hearing a spokesperson for the company defending the game by claiming, "It's obvious the woman [*tied to the pole*] is enjoying it." How long would it be till Atari came out with a game like those ones where you kill zombies with guns, only with Dudley George and the OPP?

At the other end of the political spectrum, I came across an interesting ad on the Net one day, on a site called Aphrodite Recommends: Female Sexuality. It seems there is a substance being marketed out there called, simply, Native Woman. Evidently it's some sort of First Nations aphrodisiac:

> Throughout Europe this mushroom was known as *elixirium ad longum vitam*, the elixir of long life. Before the Western World discovered this treasure, the Haida First Peoples of the Queen Charlotte Islands, in what is now British Columbia, understood its primal purpose: connecting a woman to her deepest sexual identity.[8]

I must confess that I have never been to the Queen Charlotte Islands, more commonly known in Native circles as Haida Gwaii, but now I am certainly looking forward to my first trip. This type of advertising reminds me of those ads for a pain ointment product called Lakota, publicly endorsed by Floyd "Red Crow" Westerman but created and owned by a Western Canadian Métis. They promote the concept that Native people have secret ways that only now, after most of our land has been taken away, our language destroyed, our culture and belief systems obliterated, are we willing to share. The time has come to show you white people how to have a good time and not feel sore afterwards.

But perhaps nowhere has the image of the sexual Aboriginal been so appropriated, so conjured, so manipulated but embraced, than in the uncountable number of Western/historical romance novels that populate mainstream bookstores, drugstores, airports and used-book emporiums. Romance fiction is an incredibly lucrative genre, estimated to make up more than 50 per cent of paperback fiction sales. According to Lee Masterson, author of *Write, Create and Promote a Best Seller*, historical romance is one of the most successful of the eight sub-genres of romance fiction, the others being contemporary romance, fantasy romance, futuristic romance, paranormal romance, regency romance, romantic suspense, and time-travel romance.

Come on, admit it—you've picked one up. With a big muscular Indian on the cover, sweeping some poor (or lucky, depending on your perspective) white woman off her feet. You've read the back and maybe even bought one or two:

> She was a runaway wife, with a hefty reward posted for her return. And he was the best darn tracker in the territory. For the half-breed bounty hunter, it was an easy choice. His had been a hard life, with little to show for it except his horse, his Colt and his scars. The pampered brown-eyed beauty would go back to her rich husband in San Francisco, and he would be ten thousand dollars richer.
>
> But somewhere along the trail out of the Black Hills, sometime during the long star-studded prairie nights, everything changed. Now he would give his life to protect her, to hold her forever in his embrace. Now the moonlight poetry of their loving reflected in the fiery vision of the Sun Dance: She must be his . . .[9]

This is the literature of the middle-class Caucasian housewife and, to be fair, your average working-class woman, who dreams of romance and escape. In the arms of an Indian. And not just any average Indian. An über-Indian.

It is on the covers of these stylish and carefully crafted homages to interracial love that the image of the studly male Indian reaches its pinnacle. More often than not, he's got a solid square chin, an aquiline nose, chiselled brow and long, flowing raven-black hair that can tell you the direction of the prairie breeze better then any windsock. So what if these traits are noticeably lacking from most Native men of that era? The broad noses seen in photos of Sitting Bull and Geronimo, both strikingly handsome men, are not celebrated on the covers of *Song of a Warrior* or *Wild Thunder*. And the Aboriginal bodies seen in these fantasies could only come from hours in a personal gym, not to mention some careful calorie counting (it's a known fact that muskrats have a higher fat content than buffalo).

Here lies an interesting contradiction. Objectively, the men on the covers all look like white men with good tans in dim lighting. Yet the reason these books are devoured so rabidly by a faithful audience is that the readers want more than just a love story—they want one encased in exoticism, one involving a distant but still embraceable culture and environment, far removed from their own existence. It is this sense of foreignness or otherworldliness that makes these stories so enticing. Kind of like going out for Korean or Ethiopian food: it's tasty, interesting and different, but chances are that you, the consumer, will never visit the land that created the meal you are eating. Experiencing it at the local strip mall is about as close as you're gonna get.

Part of the attraction might also be our innate desire to root for the underdog. The time period in which these books take place was arguably the last flowering of Native culture in its pure form. All the world knows what came next: the Dispossessed Indian, the Tragic Indian, the Forgotten Indian. This is a way of remembering them when they were strong, proud and free. I have yet to come across a historical romance that takes place on a reserve during the Depression. It's like telling stories about a close relative who had a stroke. More often then not, the stories will be about when he was healthy and did interesting things, not about the way he is now, bedridden and slobbering.

It's also an opportunity to experience forbidden love, a culturally unallowable tryst. Only recently—and again, this is arguable—have Native/non-Native relationships been considered non-scandalous and acceptable. But a wild Indian, savage and proud with long flowing locks and a huge powerful horse between his legs (no metaphor intended)—now that's something to get hot and bothered about, especially if you live in the suburbs, have two kids (one with the flu), drive a Honda minivan and are married to an accountant who never puts the toilet seat down.

Truth be told, I know very few, if any, Native women who read these books. The relationships in the stories are not forbidden or exotic for them. They know the reality and the pain that came from the real nineteenth-century interrelations. It was not a particularly romantic time for First Nations. It was a time of massive upheaval, the perpetuation of a centuries-long cultural genocide. So I think it's safe to say—and I could be wrong, but I would hazard a guess—that the *vast* majority of patrons of this literary genre are white.

So, again, the men are Native but look remarkably white. This limits the dimensions of the unknown, providing a touchstone that is more familiar and acceptable. See the contradiction? And if the men are not fully Native, then they are half-breeds and therefore closer to white society. What could be more romantic than the outsider, someone torn between two cultures? In a random sampling of ten historical romances, five of the male protagonists were half-breeds. Injun Joe was not among them.

And their names . . . Lone Eagle, Swift Buck, Bear, Jesse Yellow Thunder, Chase The Wind a.k.a. The White Wolf, Strong

Wolf, Wolf Shadow, Jared Redwolf (the Wolf family seems to have a real thing for kidnapped white women). Traditional Native names were not always that flattering or masculine; history books will tell you of the exploits of real Indians with names like Roman Nose, Hairy Bear, Gall, Big Foot, Dull Knife, Stumbling Bear and Lame Deer. But what does reality have to do with fantasy?

The generic story usually consists of the central character, a Native or half-breed guy, who kidnaps a white woman or is hired to find a white woman kidnapped by Natives because he "knows their ways." After a chase and some adventures, he makes her fall in love with him. There are limitless variations to this template, but essentially it's the Stockholm Syndrome with a happy ending. Of course as the story progresses, there are some bridges to be built between the two cultures. Once those are constructed, the heavy panting and teepee shaking begins. Coincidently, that's how I got my prom date.

Occasionally, the white woman was also raised by Indians. For a variety of reasons she went back to her people, only to return years later in search of something. In Rhonda Thompson's *Walk into the Flame*, the female protagonist was raised by Apaches after being abandoned by her father. At the age of seventeen she returns to "civilization"; five years later, she's back. Same principle with *Wolf Shadow* by Madeline Baker, the story of Theresa Bryant, renamed Winter Rain, except that Winter Rain still lives among her adopted people. She was raised by the Lakota, and her birth parents hire Chance McCloud, "half Lakota and half white," to find her.

Also note that the women almost always have blue eyes— this seems to be a prerequisite for being kidnapped by Indians. Their hair is usually blond or red, with the occasional foray into "dark as a raven's wing." And they range in age from seventeen to no older than twenty-three or twenty-four. That seems to be their "best before" date.

A unique code of ethics also comes into play. The women are

almost always young and virgins, and if they have had sex, it's usually within a marriage to an impotent or abusive man, frequently white, from whom they are struggling to escape. The Native men, by contrast, have been quite sexually active in prior years. When push finally comes to shove (again, no pun intended), they provide a more holistic, respectful and tender form of love and sex for these women. The coupling is almost always Indian man–white woman, very seldom the other way around—ironic, because in the real world (whatever that may be), more Native women ended up with white husbands than vice versa. Champlain put it best when he said, "Our sons shall marry your daughters and henceforth we shall be one people."

These books obviously tap into a rich world of fantasy. There never seem to be any bugs. No one's hair ever needs washing, or even combing. Nobody ever has to go to the washroom. Their clothes never stink. And everyone has a full set of teeth. For that time period, these characteristics are truly fantasy.

As a Native person, how do I feel about these books? Am I insulted? No. Do I think their portrayal of Native people is dangerous? No, no more dangerous than their portrayal of all those tall, lithe, lovely, slender, curvy women that read them with their amber/grey/green/blue eyes. Does it do our culture justice? Of course not. Does it do us any harm? If anybody believes this is reality, they are more a danger to themselves than to us.

However, I prefer to think about the genre's positive influences. For the most part these books make us out to be caring, sensitive and interesting partners, far superior to all those abusive or non-existent husbands. Not to mention fabulous lovers.

It seems our secret is out.

Their love has to be written in the stars. And their passion . . . mercy is it hot!! They give new meaning to what happens in a sweat lodge. I would sure love to be Jared Redwolf's woman.[10]

A FAN OF THE BOOK *REDWOLF'S WOMAN*

NOTES

1 Quoted in Vicki Jaimez. "Sexuality and the Invasion of America: 1492–1806." Accessed October 24, 2007. http://virtualschool.edu/mon/SocialConstruction/SexualityAndInvasion.html.

2 Jaimez.

3 William Shakespeare. *The Tempest*, Act 1, Scene 2, Line 346FF.

4 Mark Twain. *The Adventures of Tom Sawyer*. New York: Penguin Classics, 1986: 185.

5 John Seelye. "Introduction." In *The Adventures of Tom Sawyer*. Mark Twain. New York: Penguin Classics, 1986: xxii.

6 Joan Dagle. "Linear Patterns and Ethnic encounters in the Ford Western." In *Ford Made Westerns*. Gaylyn Studlar and Matthew Bernstein, eds. Indianapolis: Indiana University Press, 2001.

7 Swedish Erotica: Custer's Revenge. Accessed October 24, 2007. http://www.mobygames.com/game/swedish-erotica-custers-revenge.

8 Aphrodite Recommends: Female Sexuality. Accessed October 24, 2007. http://www.aphroditewomenshealth.com/news/aphrodite_essentials_sexuality.shtml.

9 Madeline Baker. *Spirit's Song*. Wayne, PA: Dorchester Publishing, 1999.

10 Indian Romance in Series. Accessed October 25, 2007. http://www.angelfire.com/fl2/ebenway/nativeseries.html.

WHY CREE IS THE SEXIEST
OF ALL LANGUAGES

Tomson Highway

I DON'T TEACH OFTEN, but when I do, I enjoy it immensely, especially when I am called upon to lecture on the Cree language, its meaning, its character, its sound, its idiosyncrasies. And depending on what part of the country I am guest-lecturing in, the number of people fluent in the language will vary tremendously, with some being partly fluent in it, others speaking just a little, others speaking it not at all but having some comprehension and some speaking it not at all and having no comprehension. So to cover all the bases, I will frequently explain up front that, even though I may be speaking in English at any given point in time, I am actually using that English as filtered through the mind, the tongue and the body of a person who is speaking in Cree. And generally speaking, given that English is my second, if not third, language, by a mile—I am mostly successful in doing this. If I am not, I will simply ask my audience to suspend their imaginations—and their moral sense, of which more in a second—for those few seconds when my little technique fails me (which, I'm happy to report, isn't that often, thank God).

Next I will warn my students of two things. The first is that they will laugh frequently if not constantly and, what's more, laugh not lightly or politely but fiercely, giddily, insanely, hysterically, from the gut, "so get your Kleenex ready." The second is that, to return for a second to the subject of morals, they will have to be ready to drop their guard on a dime when and if I ever come anywhere near what I call "the garden," a subject I bring up often, if not almost always. And by "the garden," I mean the human body, particularly the part of it that lies closest to—and all around—what I call "the tree of knowledge," the one that stands at stiff attention, so to speak, in the middle of that garden, the garden of beauty, the garden of pleasure, the garden of joy, a garden with which we are so blessed by the Goddess—not the God but the Goddess, I have to stress. And once having given such an introduction, away I will go . . .

I will pepper my lecture—which is delivered rapid-fire, for the simple reason that the dialect of Cree that I speak is arguably the fastest in the world—liberally with such succulent remarks as "it was so hot that day that I had rosary beads of perspiration clinging to the crack of my ass." I will say, for example, that "by the time I was halfway through my description of the flavour of that muskrat (something I had to do once, in public, at one point in my life, for a reason), they were screaming for my beaver. And I wasn't even wearing it! It was upstairs, in my top drawer, cuz you see, whenever I decide to wear beaver, I generally wear nothing but top drawer, don't you?" I will say, for example, "I was so hungry, I could have eaten a woman. No, I change my mind—I was so hungry I could have eaten a man." I will say, for example, that, "up north, where I come from, when you meet a skunk and you see him turn around preparing to spray you, you whip around, drop your pants, bend over, and spray him first. And that's how you kill a skunk. In fact, that's why there are no skunks in northern Manitoba; they were all killed some time ago in just such a manner. By my uncle George who, by the way, was admired from one end of northern Manitoba to the other for his skunk-killing abilities." I will, for instance, sometimes tell them, to explain my exotic origins, that "my father was a caribou hunter. And my mother was a caribou. Which is why, to this day, I am fascinated by bestiality. I love bestiality. For those of you who feel you don't know enough about the subject, boy have you come to the right place." Then when I turn my back to the classroom to write whatever piece of information on the blackboard for their delectation, I will say (with a wink of my eye, it goes without saying), "you want me to take off my sports jacket so you can have a good look at my ass while I'm doing this?" And at the end of the lecture, I will tell them how grateful I am for their having listened to me and for having invited me in the first place—so grateful that "if I were the Governor-General, I would decorate them. That if I were the Surgeon-General, I would let them smoke. That if I were the Receiver-General, I would cancel their taxes. And that if I were the Mother-General, I would nurse them . . . except that, unfortunately, I had to leave my tits behind in Toronto. Why? No gels or liquids allowed on planes these days!" And then I will take my leave of them with the sage advice that "in order to be successful in life these days, one must always have joy in one's heart. And soap in one's hole. Oops, I mean hope in one's soul."

From my vantage point at the head of the classroom, at each and every mention of words and phrases such as "crack of my ass," "beaver," "eating a woman" and "eating a man," "bend over and spray," "bestiality," "nurse" (in the sense, of course, of lactation), "tits," "soap in one's hole," etc., I can see the "English parts" of these students cringe with discomfort, guilt and fear, if not even horror, if not even terror, outright and blatant. In other words, every time I get anywhere near those parts of the human body where sexual pleasure, or the possibility thereof, was remotely possible, they shrink back into themselves and hide. With fear and self-loathing. And, dare I say it, disgust.

But then, at certain points—and there are more and more as my lecture goes on—something else will seep through the cracks of their deeply ingrained, English-speaking veneer. Somehow they will have slipped, clandestinely, criminally, back into "the garden," if only in spurts here and there, and the Cree parts of them will laugh. And laugh so hard their faces will turn a pinky red, their eyes will disappear into slits so tiny they look like filaments. Some of them will have tears coming out of those eyes, and some of them will actually have to wipe the sweat from their foreheads from time to time because, all of a sudden, they have become so hot. And moist. Some of them, in fact, will laugh so hard they will all but pee right there in their seats. Even the idea of "lips" getting "hot" will scare the living daylights out of their English-speaking sensibilities—as in "every time I think about French cheese, my lips get hot and, God knows, I have hot lips to begin with"—but thrill them to the bone in Cree to the point where they will wiggle and shake and rattle and roll and jiggle so hard and for so long and from every fibre of their being that the whole class will start looking, to my eyes, like one gigantic washing machine on spin cycle, and I will tell them as much. And whenever I revert to the use of "proper English," those same bodies will stop moving, their faces will drop, their shoulders will droop. And, all of a sudden, it will be like we are sitting inside a United Church. Then I'll jump back to Cree, and hell will break loose all over again. And I'll go back and forth and back and forth and back and forth in this manner for an hour— church, party, church, party, church, party, outside the garden, inside the garden, outside, inside, etc.

To give this little tale another little twist, albeit one outrageous, perhaps scandalous, little twist, one time not so long ago, I emailed a group of friends in Ottawa, telling them to come to a show that I was doing in Montreal in two weeks' time and then, at the bottom, added a postscript for the one among them who was Cree and, like me, was fluent in the language. The Cree in this postscript went: "Tansi weechigi-tooroom. Montreal see-mak pees-pathi kinoo-chig-weem asichi igatchee maw keetom kamatitin." Some two weeks later, when I saw those non–Cree-speaking friends after the show in Montreal (the one Cree among them couldn't make it, as it turns out), they were all dying to know what I had said to the Cree friend, because he had refused to translate my note for them, it was that outrageous. I was horrified. To translate *that* into English? Satan would come up from the depths and drag me into hell with his pitchfork. I had to ask them not to slap me (they were all women) if I were, in fact, to translate it for them. And when they did promise me that they would, indeed, not slap me, I took the plunge. The translation of that message into English goes as follows: "All right, you stinky cunt. Drive to Montreal right away together with that old bag of yours (my Cree friend's gay lover) or I'll never fuck you again!" You see? In English, it is horrifying. It makes your hair stand on end. Your spine freezes, and something inside you goes dead. The politically correct would string me up by the balls and hang me dry for having said it. In Cree, among friends, it is hysterically, thigh-slappingly, gut-bustingly funny. Even the sexist bent of the remark is completely absent. How does one explain this phenomenon when one has to cross the frontiers of human language?

In the classroom I spoke of earlier (and not that I used this last illustration in that classroom; I wouldn't dare), we will stop to discuss it. We will stop to discuss, my students and I, why it is that, in the sensibility, even the rhythm, of one language, talking about such things as lips and beaver and ass and tits and God-knows-what is a terrifying experience, whereas in the other, it is the funnest, and funniest, most hysterical, most spectacular thing in the world. The reason, I explain, is simple. At one point in its history, one language was evicted from a certain garden because of the actions of a woman who talked to a snake and then took pleasure in eating the fruit of a certain tree that stood—pardon the expression—at stiff attention smack in the middle of that garden; the other language never was. And the other never was for the simple reason that there is no such story as eviction from any garden in the mythology of the Indian people of North America—one definition of the term "mythology" being "the sacred stories of a people"—and it therefore follows that if we were never evicted from that garden, then we are still inside it. North America, easily the most stunningly beautiful continent on earth, in other words, is, to us, a garden—a garden of beauty, a garden of pleasure, a garden of joy. All you have to do is look around you to prove it.

If you extend, moreover, that metaphor of the garden into the human corpus itself—that is, if you think of the human body as the original garden of beauty, the garden of pleasure, the garden of joy—then the English language, at one point in its history, was evicted from that body. And at that moment, the human body became a thing of evil, of ugliness, of disgust; it, and nature, became an enemy. At that moment, human language and nature became polarized. At that moment, the human body was severed forever from its own biology, its physical functions. These functions, and the organs they came from, were never to be mentioned and, if they were, there was hell to pay for the infraction. Putting it another way, the English language may live most magnificently inside the head, in the intellect, but it stops at the neck. And it stops there because that is the gate to the garden of pleasure and at that gate stands an angel with a flaming sword who will scorch your arse the moment you dare to re-enter that garden.

Conversely, the Cree language—or any North American Aboriginal language that I know of—having no such narrative in its "sacred book," was therefore never cut off from nature or from the human body. In Cree, the relation between nature and humankind has a completely different dynamic; for us, for one thing, nature is not an enemy but a friend, an ally. This fact is why in Cree, and in other Native languages, speaking of sex and the natural functions of the human body is not verboten. It is allowed. In fact, the very nature of the language encourages it. Why? Because those functions and those organs are hysterically funny. To backtrack just a little, in one language, sex may be the dirtiest, filthiest, most evil activity the human body is capable of. In the other, it is not only the funnest, it is also the funniest. In the Cree language, the "tree of knowledge" that stands at stiff attention smack in the middle of the garden, which is the human body in all its pleasurable capacities, together with the attendant "fruit" that hangs from that tree, are not only the most ridiculous-looking objects you have ever seen with your two eyes, but they are also the most entertaining, the most beautiful, and are capable, moreover, of giving our "biological realities" the most heavenly feeling known to woman, man or beast: the orgasm. This tree, this red-hot centre of the human corpus, in other words, is capable of sending our bodies straight into heaven to commune face to face with God, whatever form that being may take in one's spirit and imagination. In other words, one system of thought, and the language that goes with it, denies biology; the other embraces it.

Another mythology—one of many—that doesn't have a story of eviction from a garden is that of the ancient Greeks, who made room in their collective subconscious for a goddess of love, of physical pleasure, of sexual delight, of death by orgasm—a deity named Aphrodite. Aboriginal mythology has its own goddess/god that stands for the exact same thing. The Trickster is the central figure in the collective North American Aboriginal dream world, i.e., in North American Aboriginal mythology, i.e., in the "sacred book" of our people. And before we dip ever so briefly, and therefore way too simplistically, into the character of this extraordinary creation of the human imagination, three essential points must be known about her/him: (1) because the language itself has no gender, she/he has none, (2) like a sort of spiritual silly putty, she/he is forever changing shape so that, in theory at least, she/he can, at one moment, be female, the next moment, male and (3) she/he is, first and foremost, a clown, a clown who laughs loudly, constantly, hysterically, from the gut, and one, therefore, who represents here on earth a god who laughs—or, pardon me, a goddess who laughs—a deity who has, horrors, a sense of humour, one whose purpose for putting human life on this planet is to let it have a good time, let it have a good belly laugh fifty times a day minimum. According to the structure of this latter "collective subconscious," namely the North American Aboriginal, the reason for existence on planet earth is not suffering or guilt (for something we never even did ourselves in the first place) but pleasure, to have one hell of a good time, to celebrate.

So although in one language, humankind is forbidden to eat the fruit of the Tree of Knowledge, in the other it is not only permitted, it is encouraged. That is precisely what that goddamn tree is there for, for humankind to suck from its fruit, and suck and suck and suck and suck, thirty times a day if necessary. That way, your body is that much more relaxed, if not euphoric, if not even exhausted, with pleasure. That way, your body is not stressed out and as tense as a steel trap meant for a bear. That way, you are that much less likely to rape a woman, beat your wife to death, start a war. Or ass-fuck pretty little eight-year-old Cree boys.

Igwani igoosi, niweecheewaganuk.*

---

* And that's it for now, my friends.

LEARNING TO SKIN
THE BEAVER

In Search of Our Aunties' Traplines

Nancy Cooper

IT'S FEBRUARY, and I'm stranded at the Winnipeg airport. I'm hoping that soon I'll be on my way to Kenora and then on to Fort Frances, to visit the Native alternative high schools in those communities. I am living the story of the modern-day Aboriginal woman traveller, as comfortable in twin props as she is in jumbo jets. Fits right in at the Tim Hortons in Kenora or at a café in Vancouver. This is the modern-day Aboriginal lesbian, as comfortable at home with Mom and Auntie as she is hanging out at a dyke event in the latest "it" club in downtown Toronto. Sounds easy, doesn't it?

But where and how do we learn to traverse these two worlds when so many of us come from isolated reserves or from places and families that don't provide us with a reflection of who we are as Native lesbians? How can I be a strong Native lesbian when I don't know where I come from? What is the history of Native lesbians in this place called Canada? Is it true that we didn't exist before contact with the "white man," as I've unfortunately heard one too many times? Where are the elders who carry the teachings about our roles and responsibilities as important, integral members of our community? Who are our "elder aunties," the ones who paved the gay way for us, the ones whose job, whether they want it or not, is to educate and inform our communities about the realities of being Native women and lesbians?

Alice Walker went in search of her mothers' gardens, looking for the seeds of creative spirit passed down from her great-great-grandmother's time. But we're different—we need to go in search of our aunties' traplines, watching and learning about all of the ways to survive as Native women, as lesbians and as members of various communities. How do we learn to skin the beaver, metaphorically speaking?

In this essay I'm going to write about my personal journey in search of my aunties' traplines. I want to show you the beauty, strength and chutzpah of my community. I want to share with you the laughter and pain and growth in my community. I'd like you to get to know some of the amazing people in my community who are role models, mentors, leaders and tricksters. Those who teach and guide the rest of us as we learn about what it really means to be Native and queer and how the two do not need to be mutually exclusive. I want you to meet some of my aunties. But, a caveat: it is still not safe for many women to be out and queer in their communities. Homophobia or lesbophobia is an ugly reality in many places in the world, and Native communities are no exception. So I'll only use some names. For others, well, you'll just have to use your imagination. Maybe I'm writing about you!

> Woman
> will you come with me moving
> through rivers to soft lakebeds
> Come gathering wild rice with sticks
> will you go with me

down the long waters smoothly shaking
life into our journey
Will you bring this gift with me
We'll ask my brother to dance on it
until the wildness sings

CHRYSTOS

Be still my beating heart! There are those among us who have used Chrystos's poetry to pick up, break up and make up with lovers over the years. I was introduced to her work by my first girlfriend, a beautiful Newfoundlander with eyes like the sea, who wrote "woman, will you come with me moving through rivers to soft lake beds" in a card to me. I was hooked . . . on girls and on Chrystos.

As a poet and an activist, Chrystos has provided many of us, queer and straight alike, with the tools to fight oppression, challenge racism, understand and accept our identities and stand up, unflinching, before injustice. In fact, my partner (a sexy Saskatchewan Métis) says that it was Chrystos's poetry that helped her survive in medical school. But Chrystos has also gifted us with the words and phrases we need to woo lovers, make it through breakups and get it on in very sexy ways: "Sheet lightning between my legs as you give me your hot coffee look." She has reflected back to us our Aboriginal queer identity in a wonderful, loving and, oftentimes, erotic way.

Her amazing volume of erotic poetry, *In Her I Am*, is one steamy book—a book that celebrates love between women, especially love between Native women. "Your soft arms shining brown over me turning/me wild in your hands/a flying lake you drank/flowers in your eyes/as I shouted too loudly coming/open." It was here, in the lines of these poems, that I learned about butches, love, lust and the beauty of other women. Chrystos's writing is also a strong reminder for us to remember and respect those who came before us, those Native butches and *femmes* who fought for a space to live and love during times that were not friendly to lesbians or gays.

TEN SEXY NATIVE LESBIAN FACTS

Did you know that one of us is . . .
- A stand-up comedian who used to practice law?
- A playwright whose latest play is written totally in Ojibway?
- Legal counsel for her First Nation?
- A world-renowned doctor and scientist?
- One of the founding members of the oldest feminist theatre company in North America?
- A former Ms. Leather Toronto?
- One of the most powerful political players in Indian Country?
- One of the best stage managers for Aboriginal theatre and dance in Canada?
- An actor and a documentary filmmaker?
- Your mother, your sister, your daughter, your best friend, your granny?

ANNUAL TWO-SPIRIT GATHERING

Every summer, for five days in the heat of August, there exists a place like no other. It is a place where Native lesbians and gays can go and just be. It is a place where they can be Native and queer and not have to be ashamed or hide any part of themselves. Each year the Annual Two-Spirit Gathering is held somewhere in Canada or the U.S. The location is chosen when a group from a certain area offers to host the next year's gathering. This is a time for visiting, participating in ceremony, making new friends, gossiping, relaxing, hooking up and learning about our roles and responsibilities. But for me, it is most especially a time to laugh and hang out with my aunties.

The aunties come and laugh and cry and stay up late, sharing stories of new love and old love and lost love, of family and of politics. The aunties gladly dispense advice and eagerly wait to hear the stories of your year. I soon learned that *the* place to be was in the aunties' cabin, where it seemed no one got any sleep and there were always tricks and pranks being pulled. The aunties can be a pretty saucy lot when they want to be. The year I went to the gathering in New Brunswick was the year that the aunties decided that everyone would get a beaver print, a lovely painted print with—well, you get the picture. Their laughter heals and infuses my heart with spirit and the tenacity to continue to love and live in the ways I choose as a strong Native lesbian. And I've still got my beaver print somewhere.

The first year I went to a gathering was in the summer of 1994, in Kansas. My girlfriend at the time, a stunning Cree woman (she's still stunning; we're just not together anymore), were in awe that such a place existed, and we soaked up the atmosphere. We learned to do beadwork, picked and prepared sweetgrass for the very first time, cooked and took pictures and watched as many of the forty other participants opened up and blossomed with character and personality because they were in a safe place where their culture and sexuality were not at odds with one other. In talking circles we shared and listened to the others tell stories from their parts of the world, learning about one another in the ancient way.

It was at that Kansas gathering that I first met Beverly Little Thunder, a beautiful Lakota woman who spent most of her time beading and visiting. She is a well-known queer activist in the Minneapolis–St. Paul area and in 2001 was the first Native American to be a grand marshal for a pride parade. She has led a lesbian sun dance for many years. She started the sun dance after she was asked to leave another sun dance because of her sexuality. A maverick, she is not without her detractors, who do not look favourably upon her decision to provide a ceremonial place for those who had been denied that place in the past.

A year went by.

In that year I lost my father, who was only in his mid-sixties when he died. My father was cremated, and I kept some of his ashes with me as I travelled. That year the gathering was in New Brunswick, hosted by the very hospitable Mi'kmaq. My girl-friend and I, and my father's ashes, drove from Ontario and set up camp for the week. One of the best parts of the gathering happens on the first night when the talking/sharing circle takes place. That year the circle had at least sixty people, and we stayed up late into the night talking around the fire and catching up. When it came my turn to speak, I told the story of losing my father but said that he was always with me. Unbeknownst to me, Beverly, who was there again that year, scoured the camp for a tiny jam jar for my father's ashes and spent every spare moment beading it with beautiful orange and white and blue beads. She presented it to me on the last day. It was one of the most touching moments in my life. I still have that jam jar, and my father has travelled all over the world with me, from Haida Gwaii to Australia.

Please find out when and where the next Two-Spirit Gathering will be held and plan to attend. Financial help is almost always provided for those needing some assistance.

AUNTIE, TELL ME A STORY

Who doesn't love a good story? As Native people, we're pretty much renowned for our storytelling abilities. Stories play an important part in our lives. And some of us are amazing story-tellers who keep 'em coming back for more. One of my aunties is like that. I could listen to her stories for hours. But these are not ordinary stories . . . these are "back in the day" lezzie stories. These are amazing but true tales from her many queer years as the gal about town. Name a major city in pretty much any country, and she'll tell you a great story about the gay bars or the lesbian subculture there. Provincetown? She's been there. San Francisco? Ditto. New York? Yup. Paris? Natch. Rome? Gotcha.

And each city is fodder for great stories that I could listen to over and over again.

One of my favourites is her story of waiting to get into the Clit Club in New York. A huge lineup didn't deter her and her friends from trying to gain access. She sauntered up to the bouncer (a very handsome butch, I'm told) and shook her hand and whispered in her ear, "Remember, we're from Canada." After they stopped shaking hands, the bouncer was in possession of a US$50 bill, and my auntie and her friends were being whisked into the bar. Years later, she returned to the club, and the bouncer—a different handsome butch—yelled out, "Hey Canada, come on in!" and they were able to bypass the line yet again. It seems that the story of the Canadians had been passed down from bouncer to bouncer, and my auntie had become part of the Clit Club lore. So the next time you are in New York City and find yourself in line at the world-famous lesbian bar, mention to the bouncer that you are a Canadian and see what happens.

Other famous stories of hers include the time she lived in a house in Toronto with three different apartments whose other occupants were Carole Pope and Lorraine Segato. How's that for a story of lesbian royalty? Or how about the one when she was in Buffalo and she coined the phrase, "White may be all right, and Black is beautiful, but Red is best in bed"? That weekend, all the girls wanted to know who this Red was! Brings a whole new meaning to the phrase *red power*, doesn't it? This auntie is also known for using the word *boobing* instead of *cruising*. Think about it.

WHO'S ON OUR SIDE?

No story of Native lesbian reality would be complete without stories of our allies, those men and women—our friends, family members, elders and co-workers—who are cool and stand side by side with us. Our being queer is not a big deal to them; instead we all make up part of the whole community. I have many aunties and uncles who fit this bill. But my favourite story of the power of alliance is about my mom, Madeline, whose heart has the constant capability of expanding to include one more person to love. After my girlfriend came out to her mother, she was immediately disowned. Needless to say, this experience was very traumatic for her, and for me. When I told my mother about it she got very angry, not understanding how any parent could do such a thing. The next time my girlfriend and I went to visit my mother, I went into the house first, as usual, and held out my arms to get a hug from my mom. But she pushed me aside and went straight to my girlfriend, grabbed her and said, "you are my girl now." There wasn't a dry eye in the house. That was more than ten years ago, and she is still a large part of my family—we exchange cards and gifts at birthdays and holidays, even though we aren't together anymore. A happy postscript to this story is that my girlfriend and her mother did make up, and they are close today.

BEING AN ALLY IS SEXY! FIVE THINGS YOU CAN DO

- Don't be afraid to challenge people when they say or do something that is homophobic.
- Ask where the queer representation is when you are at an arts event.
- Support local youth groups that are inclusive of all youth.
- Keep an open mind, and never assume someone is straight.
- Support queer filmmakers, artists and authors.

I'VE FELT INVISIBLE in the past when I've heard elders say that gays and lesbians didn't exist before contact with Europeans. It's been hurtful, especially because we are taught to listen and learn from our elders, since they carry the teachings of the people. But for every traditional person or elder who might make a disparaging or ignorant remark there is also one who carries teachings, who accepts you as you are or who knows of another person you can visit to learn more about our past and our roles.

One such elder is my auntie Maria Campbell. Best known for her novel *Halfbreed*, this Métis elder is a living whirlwind of creativity. She currently works as a professor, a playwright, a writer and a researcher, just to mention a few of her gifts. Several of her adopted nieces and nephews are lesbian and gay. She provides guidance to many of us and isn't afraid to provide us with swift metaphorical kicks to the behind when she feels we deserve them. I've been fortunate to participate as a peripheral helper in ceremonies with her on the land and have learned a lot from her and the other old people she works with. Her guidance and love have helped many of us throughout the years.

These elders are out there, just waiting for us to come to them and ask for their ideas, input and opinions, many of which might surprise you. Just remember that old saying—"When the student is ready, the teacher appears." When you are ready with your questions and know why you want to know what you want to know, the elders will appear. Just have your tobacco ready.

I've been fortunate enough in this life to become friends with many of these amazing women. Their strength, humour, sadness and capacity for continued growth have shown me the many and varied paths of their traplines. Traps set with loving care, for those who follow to be fed and clothed with gifts from the earth and from the heart. They have left snares low to the ground under the brush to capture love and forgiveness. They have left caches full of bravery and empathy. We follow the trails they have cut through the wilderness, making it clearer and easier for us to go on our way and make use of these magnificent gifts. It's been because of their words, actions and realities that many of us from the "younger" generation have been able to claim our rightful place in our communities of choice, be they in cities or at home. Thank you to Chrystos, Beverly, Maria and all the others who have helped me on my journey time and time again. Thank you, elder aunties. I think you're all pretty damn sexy!

THE DARK SIDE OF SEX

Marius P. Tungilik

I AM AN INUK and was born in 1957 in Repulse Bay—
then part of the Northwest Territories and now part
of Nunavut. I served as the first deputy minister of Nunavut's
Department of Human Resources, a deputy minister intern
for the Northwest Territories with the Department of Renewable Resources, the senior government official for the Keewatin
Region (now commonly known as the Kivalliq) and a store manager, among many other roles in the private and public sectors.
In addition, I chaired the Nunavut Arbitration Board and was
president of the Inuit Non-Profit Housing Corporation, the
safe shelter for the Keewatin Region, the regional emergency
response committee and the crisis line. I now work as a freelance
interpreter and translator and work part-time at the municipal
office. I have two children, and I have married and divorced
twice. I enjoy hunting, fishing, camping, travelling, reading and
spending time with family and friends. I am also a victim of child

sexual abuse and have for many years played a lead role in exposing the sordid legacy of residential schools. I hope that this essay will provide some insight into Inuit heritage and also to some of the challenges we face with the darker side of sex.

Being victims or survivors of child sexual molestation in residential school was something that we did not talk about for decades after it happened. When we were kids, we did not possess the language to express how we felt. We simply did not have the words yet. As we got older, the issue became too shameful and complicated to even begin to talk about. However, because it was an unresolved childhood trauma, many of us coped with it in many dysfunctional ways, from family violence, misdirected anger, addiction to drugs or alcohol and compulsive behaviour such as gambling to, sadly for some, a perpetuation of the cycle of abuse. Individual or group therapy is not readily available in the isolated Arctic. The lack of professional resources and the extremely high cost of travel are barriers for us.

As a survivor myself, I still cannot sleep in the dark, unless I have no choice. I remember my first attempts of speaking about what I had to go through in school. I could not talk about it without sobbing uncontrollably. The feelings and emotions were much too strong. I felt that I might die just talking about it. I think many survivors felt exactly the same way. We had kept all of it a dirty secret for more than twenty or thirty years. And many therapists and counsellors did more harm than good because they refused to believe that members of the church would actually be involved in abusing small children sexually and had no idea how to deal with the issue. It became clear that abuse in residential schools was one of the best kept secrets among Aboriginal peoples.

In the late 1980s I decided that I had to publicly disclose the legacy of abuse in residential schools. With the help of my friends Peter Irniq and Jack Anawak, both of Ottawa, Ontario, I organized a meeting of residential school abuse victims in 1992 to begin to address the effects of abuse in a real public sense. For many survivors, it was the first time that they could finally talk about the trauma they suffered as children. Over the course of the next few years, I heard many horror stories from former students across the country. We launched a criminal investigation, negotiated public apologies from the governments and the churches, advocated the formation of healing institutes and launched major lawsuits.

The healing has begun, but for many it is a lifelong struggle. There are simply too many complexities to deal with at once. However, opening up about feelings associated with the effects of being assaulted in a sexual way at such a tender age is the way to start living a better life. When we initially brought up the topic of residential schools in a public forum, we were met with a tremendous amount of resistance, mainly because people found it hard to believe that we actually went through the experience that we claimed we had and because it was the first time that many had heard such talk. Yet, we knew that we could not just give up, because something had to be done.

There are many steps on the road to recovery and healing. Acknowledgement of what happened is important. Apologies for what should not have happened are also needed. Charging the people who committed the crimes and making them face justice help to confirm for us that we were not at fault. Telling our stories and holding public inquiries are vital so that more people will be aware of the dark history of Canada. Fair and equitable financial compensation is something that we continue to fight for—civil litigation to hold those responsible for the damage and harm done may not be possible. One cannot put a price on lost lives, but we feel that there should be penalties to deter future harmful action.

The criminal investigation conducted by the RCMP into the case at my school disappointingly did not result in any charges.

Some of the guilty parties had died, and the prosecutor's office of the Northwest Territories felt that the others were too old to ever do such unspeakable harm anymore. The prosecutor also added that some incidents were "minor in nature," a claim that prompted public outcry. In our case, no one was arrested or served any time in jail. The abusers did not even have to appear before a judge or jury for what they had done to us. So much for criminal justice.

However, Yellowknife lawyer Katherine Peterson conducted an independent review that the Government of the Northwest Territories commissioned, and it concluded that what we had presented was true and recommended a number of actions, including launching awareness campaigns and increasing government funding to community-based support networks. At least through that review we felt validated. Perhaps the upcoming Truth and Reconciliation Commission will bring more positive results. I am looking forward to that process.

When we began telling our stories, we wanted to make it clear that sexual molestation and sexual abuse or assault are not acceptable and would not be tolerated. We did not want people to be silent about these matters anymore, even if it meant that former students who had been abused were incarcerated for abusing children sexually. We wanted people to know that there would be no exceptions. It was the only way to end the cycle of violence and silence.

The abuse did not just affect us—it had an intergenerational impact. Because we had been quiet about our experience as children, and because we coped with life's difficulties in a dysfunctional manner for such an extended period of time, our behaviour and suffering affected how our children dealt with life. Unintentionally we had passed on many undesirable traits and characteristics to our children—including feelings of misdirected anger and addictive behaviour. Therefore, the younger generation also requires help. It is difficult, if not impossible, for survivors to talk about the abuse they suffered as children to their own offspring. Yet they need to know. They need the tools to learn new skills to cope with life in a positive way.

Confusion about parenting is a major issue for survivors of residential schools. Do we grant our children more freedom because of the fact that we suffered from too much discipline as we grew up? Or do we try to control them and provide as much structure as possible so that they will not have to go through the same things we did? We had spent much of our childhood away from our parents because of our time in residential school.

I found out when I spoke with some of the nuns that took care of us for nine months of the year at the hostel that they thought we were orphans or had been taken away because our families mistreated us at home. What a contrast from the truth! We were so loved and cherished at home, but because our parents held the church in such high regard, we could not talk to them about the ugly things that happened to us at school. Our parents would instruct us to listen to and obey the nuns, brothers and priests there. They had no idea that these people were monsters who preyed on innocent children. At the time, running away from school was out of the question because of the vast distance from home and the cold climate. And the people who were entrusted to care for us had no regard for human life. They could do whatever they wanted to us, and they knew it. All the while that they preached the gospel and spoke of godly things, they abused us physically, sexually, emotionally, spiritually and culturally.

The federal government's policy of assimilating Aboriginal peoples into mainstream white society did not do anything to help our cause. We were expected to become little white boys and girls. We were forbidden from and punished for speaking our language in school. Although we received a good education in English, we were made to feel shameful of our Native heritage.

As a result, some of us lost our language, lost cultural values and generally became confused about identity. We felt inferior to whites. At home, because we lost out on cultural teachings at a critical age, we felt inferior to Inuit as well.

Before I was taken away from my parents to school at the age of five, my family discussed sexuality openly, as I recall. They talked about it both jokingly and seriously. They warned us about incest, sexual relations with animals, rape or sexual assault and sexual relations with close relatives. Sometimes, they clearly had fun joking about sex. After our experience with sex as children and because of the religious perimeters that the missionaries established, sex was hard to talk about or not discussed at all.

When I was young, many Inuit had marriages arranged at birth or shortly afterward. These arrangements were based on the premise that everyone should have a partner in life because it was so difficult for a single person to survive in such harsh conditions. One of the factors considered in choosing a future spouse for a child was the compatibility of the parents of the children in question, since it would be easier to resolve conflicts if the parents and in-laws got along. Many wives have told me that they did not want to get married and simply did not love their husbands at first. In many cases, however, they confided that their love for their spouse grew very strong over the years. There are very few cases of divorce within arranged marriages.

Traditionally, Inuit couples had clearly defined roles in order to survive and to get along with each other. Women had the task of caring for and teaching children. In addition, they cooked, sewed, dressed animal skins, gathered heather for cooking and tended to the *qulliq* (stone oil lamp), among many other tasks. Men made and maintained hunting, trapping and fishing equipment such as spears, sleds, dog harnesses and spearheads; harvested wildlife; fed and took care of the huskies; built igloos and inuksuit. Men and women had to co-operate with each other. They also shared food and other essential items with others willingly.

Couples were expected to have children. If they could not bear children or if someone in the community could not care for their own, custom adoption—a special provision to allow Inuit to adopt children without having to go through the normal channels of law—was and still is the norm. Unlike our neighbours to the south, however, the children know who their biological parents are and maintain a close relationship with them.

In earlier times Inuit played some games that were sexual in nature. Although I am not an expert by any means, because these games have not been played for many years now, there was a game called *amaruujaq* (the wolf game). Men and women chased each other outdoors, after dark. What they did when they caught one another, I can only imagine. I am not sure if these games will ever be revived. In a way, I wish there were a way to bring them back. They are a part of our culture that has been lost. I am sure there were other games that I am not aware of.

Inuit throat singing is another source of entertainment that can be very erotic and sexually simulating, depending on the style of throat singing and the intent of the songs. Clearly, some of throat singing is solely for non-sexual entertainment. But, in some instances, it can serve to excite people in a very sexual way.

Today, relationships and our roles in the community are harder to define. It is not uncommon for couples to meet in bars or parties—rather than at feasts and other community gatherings—with varied results. Rather than have arranged marriages, people are free to marry whomever they want according to the modern notions of love. In many cases a marriage is based on physical attraction rather than compatibility or personal traits. Needless to say, the number of separations and divorces is much higher now, and single parenting is more common. And in the wake of the women's liberation movement and other modern notions of equality, roles between genders are harder to define or assign. Although some Inuit women may feel disadvantaged in some ways, men have clearly lagged behind in terms of employment and training in the North. Far more women than men are taking training programs or pursuing advanced education, and more women are employed than men. Still, far more men are involved in politics than women. For some, a double income has meant prosperity. Extended family living arrangements, although not quite as common anymore, still exist.

FOR ME, SEX can be a hard topic to discuss, but because I was one of the very first to publicly disclose the abuse at residential schools, I feel that I have a duty to listen to people and to work relentlessly to bring about resolution to the issues involved. It is a price I have to pay for leading the way to make sure that no one is left behind. Do I get tired of it? Absolutely. Do I suffer from alcohol addiction and other afflictions as a result of my role as leader in this regard? Absolutely. But, in so many ways, I find it very rewarding to help others start and continue on the difficult journey to recovery. And so, I will stay and fight as hard as I can for as long as I can for social justice. I will continue to speak out and give voice to those who need assistance. Hopefully, I will have fewer personal problems in the process than I have had in the past.

Although forgiveness is an essential part of healing, I did not find it easy to forgive my abusers. It is difficult in best of times. To have a sense of peace or indifference for such a traumatic experience is hard to achieve. Some people have no idea what we had to go through. It has not been easy by any means, but now far more people are opening up and far more are aware of the legacy than ever before. There is still a lot to do, but it is easier now because more people speak of the need to heal. As human beings, we all suffer from some pain, and we all need to get on with our life in some way. After all, it is not normal to constantly and persistently live in the past.

Sex is a natural part of humanity, and I enjoy it as much as anyone else, I believe. There is, after all, a world of difference between good, healthy sex and sex that is dark and abusive. In an environment where one can feel safe and loved, the dark side of sex is nowhere to be seen. It is not even something that I think about in the slightest. I have reason to believe that everyone feels exactly the same way no matter what their past.

I was not at all sure if I could write about these subjects at first, but I am glad that I have. I owe a world of thanks to Peter Irniq and Jack Anawak, as well as to my family, for the support they have provided me over the years, and I am thankful to the editor of this book for the opportunity to voice my feelings. More victims of abuse need to write and share their stories so that people will have a better appreciation into our plight and predicament. Sharing can be therapeutic as well.

Me sexy? Ask me. I certainly think I am.

NORVAL MORRISSEAU
AND THE EROTIC

Michelle McGeough

*N*ORVAL MORRISSEAU'S CONTRIBUTIONS to the art world are monumental. As the founder of the Woodlands school of painting, and with a career spanning five decades, he has exerted an influence visible in the artwork of generations of Aboriginal artists. Throughout his career he has consistently created and added to a body of erotic work, but critics and curators have largely ignored this facet of his artistic practice. Historically, Aboriginal people did not consider the erotic as a separate category of expression as it is within the Euro-Canadian artistic tradition. Rather, oral traditions often incorporated what Europeans considered erotic elements. Morrisseau's depictions of the Anishnaabe oral traditions early in his career reflect his awareness of this traditional approach.

It is difficult to determine how many erotic works by Morrisseau exist. He was by all accounts a prolific painter, especially in his early years as an artist,[1] but he has explored both the female and male nude throughout his career. These works raise some very interesting questions regarding the ideologies and assumptions that the depiction of the nude embodies. Norval Morrisseau's erotic imagery makes visible notions of the body, sexuality and gender in a very different way compared with the imagery of the nude by mainstream male artists and therefore unmasks and challenges the authority of western European sensibilities.

By examining key Western theories, such as those of Michel Foucault and Roland Barthes, what becomes evident is that the depictions of the nude by Western male artists are historical constructs and reflect a particular world view. By juxtaposing Morrisseau's interpretation of the nude, I reveal how his depictions are capable of revealing a different understanding—one rooted firmly in an Anishnaabe world view.[2]

Michel Foucault's work on the construction of sexuality and gender offers a particularly important basis for comparing Western and Anishnaabe perspectives. Foucault writes in the *History of Sexuality* that prior to the rise of the middle-class bourgeoisie the ruling class justified its control and power by forming alliances; one's power was determined by one's bloodline.[3] Controlling sex was a way for the middle class to mark and maintain its distinctiveness from other classes and ensure its health and longevity. As the middle class rose to power in Europe in the seventeenth century it seized command, owing to its interest in self-affirmation and preservation, of the control over life and death that the aristocratic lord formerly held over his vassals. Sex became something to approach calmly and study rationally and to analyze and classify. Sexuality became regulated, as Foucault states, in four areas: in children, in women, in married couples and in the sexually "perverse."[4] Foucault writes: "The society that emerged in the nineteenth century ... put into operation an entire machinery for producing true discourse concerning it [and] also set out to formulate the uniform truth of sex."[5] This development resulted in a prescriptive delineation of the kinds of sensations and pleasures that were permissible and not permissible as well as specific definitions of gender and sexuality, classification systems also reflected in the judicial system's differentiation between the pornographic and the erotic. Although the definitions of each have been legally challenged and revised over the years, and although in the contemporary period we are increasingly made aware that what is considered an affront in one community may not be one in another, community standards continue to be a decisive factor in distinguishing the erotic from the pornographic.

Although Foucault's analysis does not represent the most recent theorization of sexuality, and although it has been criticized as being "scrupulously ethnocentric"[6] because of its failure to address issues of race and gender, his arguments are important because they continue to inform much contemporary theory and because his insights into the development of sexuality in early Western societies are relevant to the notions of sexuality, the body and gender brought to the Anishnaabe by Roman Catholic missionaries. As anthropologist Ann Laura Stoler points out, these notions were inextricably bound to the imperial project; ruling colonies "entailed colonizing bodies and minds."[7] For Aboriginal people in North America the residential school was one of the most invasive tools used to eradicate traditional Aboriginal beliefs and practices. Many Aboriginal children who attended residential schools were subjected to emotional and physical abuse. Some, including Norval Morrisseau, were also sexually abused,[8] and this traumatic experience may be reflected in Morrisseau's treatment of erotic themes in his art.

For a Western perspective philosopher Roland Barthes illuminates the process by which mythologies change and how ideology becomes naturalized or ingrained into a culture. In

Mythologies, Barthes writes, "Myth hides nothing and flaunts nothing: it distorts: myth is neither a lie nor a confession: it is an inflexion. The principle function of myth is to transform history into nature."[9] His theorization is very useful in explaining how ideologies of the middle class have been generated and reinforced through popular culture and in particular demonstrate how the nude embodies and bolsters middle-class ideologies regarding the body, sexuality and gender. Although Barthes's theories are based on his observations of post-war France, his insight into the role that mass media plays in propagating the values and beliefs of the middle class remains relevant.

Such Western perspectives underscore the differences between Morrisseau's understanding regarding the body, gender and sexuality and that of his mainstream peers, as manifested in his depiction of the nude, whether it be the female nude, the male nude or the androgynous.

THE FEMALE NUDE

As Lynda Nead observed in *The Female Nude: Art, Obscenity and Sexuality*, "More than any other subject, the female nude connotes art . . . it is the icon of western culture, a symbol of civilization and accomplishment."[10] Yet the depiction of the female form throughout Western history has come under scrutiny for various reasons.

In the past century the debate about depictions of the female form has ranged from differentiating between the nude and the naked to examining and questioning the power and politics inherent in depictions of the female form within a patriarchal society. The latter signaled a departure from the neo-Kantian argument that works of art are not affected by political or social realities. Since the 1960s much of the discussion regarding the representation of the female form has examined how artistic practices and art institutions are "implicated in the production and reproduction of sexual positions in a way that manage desire and pleasure, fuel fantasies and situate the viewer."[11]

As Foucault pointed out, with the rise of the middle class, power was deployed through sexuality in a number of ways. What occurred in the Western world was that a sexual hierarchy that "asserts the primacy of the masculine over the feminine"[12] was established, along with specific constructed definitions of gender and sexuality.

Studying Morrisseau's artwork allows us to explore whether it is possible for a male artist from a different culture to produce a different understanding of female sexuality through his depiction of the female nude. If so, what does that say with regard to the authority of a patriarchal sexual hierarchy and its myths regarding women's sexuality?

The inspiration Morrisseau gained from the Anishnaabe legends he heard as a child and as an adult is clearly evident in his depiction of the nude or semi-nude female form, which was not restricted to the human form.[13] As Overholt and Callicott observed in their inquiry into Anishnaabe legends:

> They mirror a series of complex interrelationships among a variety of kinds of persons: spirits and men, spirits and animals, spirits and spirits, men and men, men and animals, men and inanimate objects ... also that animals are said to possess what we would normally consider to be human qualities: they can speak and plot complicated strategies and they have human emotions.[14]

Although their omission of women in this passage reflects the androcentricity of the 1980s, the authors' observations reveal the relation between animals and humans in the Anishnaabe world view. Morrisseau often revisited these subjects and themes, producing not just one painting but several representations of women that include Mother Earth and the Mother of All Serpents, as well as the human female nude. Although Morrisseau, like Western artists, produces images depicting the female nude, a different understanding of the world and of women inspires his iconography.

WOMEN AS NATURE

Equating woman and nature became symbolic of what man must control and overcome if he is to transcend and evolve. Within the construct of Cartesian dualism, women were associated with the body, emotion, the primitive and animality and were thus diametrically opposite to man and reason. Beginning with the scientific revolution, Western society no longer saw itself as belonging to the natural world and began divorcing itself from any dependence on the biosphere. In doing so, "Western society denied women's activity and indeed the whole sphere of reproduction."[15] Women and nature became what eco-philosopher Val Plumwood describes as the background to which all men's activity took place.[16] This perspective is particularly evident in the depiction of the female nude. Although women were often depicted as passive, the patriarchal society feared that women's civility was only a pretense. Within the Western artistic tradition the female nude is depicted as submissive and passive—a projection of the phallocentric desire to control and contain women's sexuality—or she is depicted in such a way that she embodies patriarchy's fear of female power.

In contrast, Morrisseau's painting *Mother Earth* (1975) (see fig. 1) exemplifies some very different notions regarding the association between earth, women and the feminine.[17] In this acrylic-on-canvas painting from a private collection, a female form is depicted in Morrisseau's characteristic combination of frontal view with a side facial profile. On a background of brilliant red his black arabesque formlines separate the elements from each

Figure 1. MOTHER EARTH

1975, 104 cm × 203.2 cm, Acrylic on canvas, Private collection, Reproduced from Lister
Sinclair and Jack Pollock, *The Art of Norval Morrisseau*, p. 124.

other while also indicating the interconnection among them. The predominant element is the image of a nude female form as indicated by her bare breasts and stylized depiction of female genitalia. She appears to be sitting cross-legged, a position that exposes her genitals, depicted as a red circle with small yellow dots. Her arms cross in front of her body, while her right hand seems to be in the process of transforming into a bird. She wears what appear to be arm- and wristbands painted in dark green that almost appears black. Around her neck she wears medicine bags of blue, black and dark green. The figure's long, black hair is worn loosely, falling over her right shoulder with earlocks on either side of her face. She wears an ornate headdress constructed of flat, opaque ovoid shapes of red, green, blue, yellow and purple.

In the upper left corner is a yellow circle outlined with a black formline and black lines radiating outward. Two of these black radiating lines connect to two human heads, both of which are shown in profile. One head is depicted with an elongated body painted blue with black formlines creating a graphic design depicting what appear to be ribs. He/she is devoid of any limbs and faces the female form. This human figure and the female form, with their beaklike mouths, appear to be conversing. On the back of the human figure are two heads, one positioned above the other, facing outward and away from the central image. This seemingly odd combination of human heads and a limbless body appears to be resting on or supported by the head of a bear. Below the bear, Morrisseau once again employs a circle motif, its contour defined by a black formline and filled with a flat, opaque medium blue colour. Similar to the other circle, three black lines emanate from the circular form joining the bear to a fish upon which the female form appears to be sitting. The graphic design of the fish illustrates what Mary Beth Southcott has described as cloisonnism[18] of deep reds, purple, greens and blues. Above the fish's tail fin and nestled beside the left leg of the mother earth figure is a bird that resembles a loon, which also demonstrates Morrisseau's use of cloisonné-like graphic treatment.

This image of Mother Earth, humans and other-than-human beings illustrates Anishnaabe notions of the connection between the earth and women and also of the interconnections marking relationships between the humans and the other-than-human beings.

WOMEN AS AUTONOMOUS SEXUAL BEINGS

Morrisseau's depiction of the human female form speaks of an active sexuality that is profoundly creative and gives us a glimpse of woman as an autonomous sexual being who is both a subject and an object of desire.

The active sexual aspect of woman is the subject of Morrisseau's painting *Woman* (c. 1960) (see fig. 2, overleaf). Painted in acrylics, this image is an example of Morrisseau's more economical use of line and detail. On a coloured background of dark and light green blocks, a nude woman is depicted in a stylized replication of a classical reclining nude pose. The female form is portrayed using a combination of a side profile with partial frontal view of her body. Her lower limbs disappear out of the frame and off the canvas. Around her neck she appears to be wearing a necklace or medicine pouch. On her face is a series of black dots—one above the other, following the outline of her cheekbone and tracing a line down towards her mouth to her chin, perhaps depicting a facial tattoo. Her arms reach underneath her knees while her hands grip her thighs as she holds open her legs to reveal her genitals. Pubic hair seems to radiate from her genitals and, as in Morrisseau's other erotic images, there are sacred dots painted on the genital area. The negative space created by thick black lines, which form her torso against the background, is painted orange instead of green, perhaps alluding to a heightened state of arousal. Resting on the figure's thigh and arm are

Figure 2. WOMAN

c. 1960, Acrylic on canvas, Reproduced from the exhibition catalogue,
Norval Morrisseau and the Development of Woodland School of Painting,
Maslak McLeod Gallery, 2000, p. 17.

two birds outlined in thick black formlines and filled with an opaque blue colour. The presence of these birds at first seems out of place. However, the eyes of the birds are composed of a circle within a circle, indicating that the birds are otherworldly.[19] They also create a focal point, countering Morrisseau's positioning of the female form and her averted gaze, which create a directional line that leads the eye away from the image. This directional line produces a feeling that there is more occurring beyond the spectator's vision, outside the picture frame, creating a tension that cannot be resolved: the viewer becomes aware that he or she can only be a spectator. In John Berger's sense as he outlines in *Ways of Seeing*, Morrisseau's *Woman* typifies the naked in that we as spectator can only witness the relationship as she presents herself and her desire for her lover. *Woman* is an expression of the figure's sexuality, not the spectator's; she is different from the nude because her will and intentions are revealed.[20]

Although Berger in *Ways of Seeing* states that the naked is free of patriarchal conventions, his statement is somewhat problematic when applied to Morrisseau's *Woman*, as this image makes what is considered private within a Western world view into something very public. As Lynda Nead points out, it is the space in which an image is viewed that differentiates between the erotic and pornographic.[21] The distinctions between public and private are not as stringent or strictly policed within the Anishnaabe community as they are in cultures influenced by Western Judeo-Christian ideologies and beliefs. Although anthropologist Ruth Landes's observations regarding the Anishnaabe written during the 1930s are laced with judgmental rhetoric, they reveal the community's attitudes of the period regarding sex.

> Promiscuous love practiced between boys and girls exists not only because of the absence of adult supervision, but also because of the general attitude in the community regarding love and sex. These are considered very enjoyable, socially and sensuously.[22]

Many of the Anishnaabe oral traditions contain a number of examples of this attitude of the community towards sex and love. Although these stories are often told by men, Landes points out that "Through the winter months older women often tell their life histories and devote a great amount of time and interest to elaborating their past affairs with lovers and husbands."[23]

Morrisseau brings this understanding to our attention in his painting *Woman*. Even if mainstream ideas regarding female sexuality have become ingrained, and what it means to be female is now defined in terms of a patriarchal social construct, *Woman* reminds us that this social construct has not always been the Anishnaabe reality. Her tattoo marks her as speaking from a different time, a time that, ironically, feminists envision for the future where "beyond her maternal roles, the mother is also a woman, a subject, with a life, sex and desires of her own."[24]

Morrisseau's depictions of the female nude in its various incarnations appear to replicate the dominant patriarchal representations of woman, but when the imagery is examined in terms of an Anishnaabe world view it reveals a different understanding and construct. Morrisseau bases much of his imagery on the legends and stories of the Anishnaabe people, stories meant not just to entertain but also to instruct the Anishnaabe on how to live. The stories are the Anishnaabe's truth, a truth in which sexuality and desire are only one aspect of a being. Morrisseau's images are like mnemonic devices that remind the Anishnaabe of a different way of knowing. They enable us to begin to unravel and question the authority of patriarchal assumptions and the social construct of woman.

MORRISSEAU AND THE MALE NUDE

Depictions of the male nude have a history dating back to antiquity, even though whenever we think of "the nude" we have a propensity to equate this term solely with the female form. This notion is probably due to the proliferation of paintings of female nudes during the last three hundred years. However, we have a tendency to forget that depicting the female nude was an anomaly prior to the rise of the middle class. As Lynda Nead points out, "in very general terms, it can be said that the unclothed male model dominated the life class in European academics and studios up until the late eighteenth century."[25] The male nude, unlike the female nude, arguably did not become an object of erotic contemplation until recently, when its value as a commodity within a consumer culture grew. Still, within patriarchal societies and even in a contemporary context, to objectify the male body is to venture into dangerous territory. On one level the male nude alludes to a recognition of the possibility of a female gaze, but according to Kenneth MacKinnon, the greater threat of the male nude is in "its revelation of the homoerotic potential surrounding the viewing of male objects."[26]

Historically, in the Western art tradition the male nude, unlike the female nude, was always "embedded in narrative, myth or allegory,"[27] thus allowing it to transcend and disavow the erotic. Concurrently, culturally sanctioned representations of ideal manhood expressed by the male nude evolved into two social constructions, which art historian Abigail Solomon-Godeau describes as "a heroic, virile and purposeful manhood understood as active and dominating, and a typically younger model—adolescent or ephebic, whose sensual and erotic appeal derives at least in part from its relative passivity."[28] Art historian Edward Lucie-Smith divides the feminized youth into subtypes that he terms the "anti-masculine male." This male nude is represented as the naked child, the pubescent youth and the androgynous being.[29] These subtypes activate discussions on a number of levels regarding male sexuality and its articulation in Western society. First, they point to a Western ideology that reduces sexuality to the dichotomous categories of heterosexuality or homosexuality. Second, these subtypes suggest the male body as an object of erotic contemplation.

Although the male nude's association with the heroic and allegorical has historically allowed it to elude erotic objectification, this is no longer always the case. In view of the feminist and gay and lesbian movements, new perspectives have arisen regarding the male nude that reveal the instability of not only the dichotomy of masculine and feminine but also their dominance.

Consequently, this new paradigm has led scholars to reexamine homo/heterosexual classifications of all sexuality. However, it is still questionable as to how far we have moved away from these social constructs, especially considering the cover photos found on men's health magazines and the flourishing of the metrosexual male. Norval Morrisseau's depiction of the male nude refuses to comply with the Western social construct of masculinity as embodied in the representations mentioned above. I contend that because his depiction of the male nude often merges and blurs the boundaries between these binaries, Morrisseau participates in what art historian Eve Kosofsky Sedgwick describes as an "endemic crisis of homo/heterosexual definitions."[30]

The male nude has a long history but has eluded recognition as an object of erotic contemplation. The arts of the Greeks and Romans attest to the eroticism of the male nude in ancient times. In fact one might venture to say that it is the only time in Western history when the male nude was openly appreciated for its eroticism.[31] The influence of fifth-century Greece is largely present in Western art, as evidenced by the established depictions of the male nude that continue to be replicated throughout history. Although Morrisseau's imagery is derived from Anishnaabe oral traditions, one gets the sense that there is a reinscription or at least recognition by Morrisseau of these archetypes. Morrisseau's images of the male nude exemplify his understanding of a "special language for the male penis" and his assertion that "it is the most sacred object in the spirit world."[32] Yet, Morrisseau's depictions always take the viewer beyond the obvious pictorial representation to layers of deeper meaning.

Morrisseau incorporates archetypes established by Western art historical conventions, as described by art historians Solomon-Godeau and Lucie-Smith, along with the original insight from basic tenets of the Anishnaabe world view. This recognition is particularly evident in his images of shamans

and mythical beings in his self-portraits. These images recall
the virile active heroic nude, a theme Morrisseau has revisited
numerous times throughout his career, as seen in *Self Portrait
of an Indian Artist* (1985) as well as a number of untitled
images from the private collection of Michele and Gabor Vadas
(Morrisseau's adopted son).

Unlike the Western heroic male whose maturity is characterized by exaggerated masculine characteristics that emphasize the
perfect male physique, Morrisseau focuses our attention on only
one part of the male physique—the penis. Morrisseau is consis-
tent in depicting the male nude with a disproportionally large
penis. In other world art, the representation of the large penis
is represented to indicate the creative powers that the male possesses. The similarities between the Anishnaabe and African
world views and the association of the phallus with fertility and its
metaphorical association with creation may have influenced Morrisseau's depiction of the large phallus. This is evident in *Untitled*
(1990s), a drawing on paper from the Vadas collection (see fig. 3,
overleaf). This image shows a single male figure in profile. He
appears to be nude with the exception of his feet, which are
coloured a solid red, a graphic treatment that may represent moccasins. The lower portions of his legs from the knee downward
are graphically treated with black horizontal lines, indicating
leggings or perhaps tattoos or paint applied onto the body. This
same graphic treatment appears on the arms, around the male figure's neck as well as the shaft of the penis. His circumcised penis
is disproportionately large and in a semi-erect state. Inside the
contour line are numerous randomly arranged small black dots.
Similar dots also appear on the shaft of the penis; however, here
the dots are arranged in an orderly fashion, one in front of the
other, perhaps indicating sperm and ejaculation. Sitting on the
shaft of his penis is a small human creature, whose hands and feet
mirror the coloured graphic treatment of the larger male figure.

Figure 3. UNTITLED

1990s, n.k., Ink on paper, Private collection of Gabor
and Michele Vadas, Nanaimo, B.C.

Several other small humanlike creatures appear to be resting on the male figure's arms—all but one is in a seated position. Each figure is shown in profile as the black contour line that outlines the eye continues vertically through the centre of the profiled body. The sex of these small beings is curiously omitted. On the head of the large central male figure, a black formline outlines a contour resembling the racks of moose antlers. These antler-like shapes appear to be fashioned from the male figure's hair as small black hatch marks indicate hair being pulled away from the scalp, which is further demonstrated by two strands of long hair curling at the base of the neck. It is difficult to determine the significance of fashioning the hair in this manner. This coif, along with the markings on the legs and arms and around the neck may be indicators of the male figure's cultural identity and nationality. However, they may also be merely symbolic, representing the qualities of endurance and strength that, according to Basil Johnston, are the traits the moose symbolizes for Anishnaabe.[33]

Along the back of the male figure are seven figures positioned, one beside the other, in a vertical line facing the viewer. I believe them to be what Morrisseau refers to as ancestral figures, as they resemble figures found in Midèwiwin scrolls and shaman petroglyphs. Three of the ancestral figures have hornlike appendages; one on either side of their heads. Like the smaller humanlike figures held by the male figure, the bear's body is divided by a thin black horizontal line that runs from the circle that forms its eye through to the tail of the animal. The black lines curl inward to create a small spiral. Three vertical lines connect each spiral to the heavy black formline that traces the contour of the bear's body. In depicting both the internal and external realities these two states are seen as being equally important. In the upper right-hand corner of the image is a butterfly.

Morrisseau's graphic treatment of the background of the image almost appears to be an afterthought. In the top two-thirds of the white background we see a single or small groups of two or three black pine or spruce trees seemingly placed to balance the composition. Directly above the nude male figure is a thin formline of red in the shape of a circle, outlined by another formline of black, with seven smaller black lines radiating outward. This small visual element depicting the sun provides the greatest insight into what I believe is Morrisseau's visual narrative about creation.

Basil Johnston explains that the circle is considered to be a sign of perfection and is employed as a visual element in Anishnaabe art to represent the Creator, Kiche Manitou. The presence of the circle reminds the viewer not only of Kiche Manitou but possibly also of the important role the sun plays in creation and sustaining life. The sun, along with the earth, is continually engaged in the process of creation, as witnessed in the changing of seasons. But more importantly Morrisseau's drawing is imbued with the theme of creation and in particular of fatherhood. The male figure's prowess and fertility are suggested by the interplay of the visual elements such as the abundance of pubic hair, the large penis and the small dots depicted on the scrotum and the shaft of the penis, which may signify sperm while also implying Morrisseau's assertion of the sacredness of the penis in the spirit world.[34]

THE ANDROGYNOUS

In contrast to the Western world view, the Anishnaabe traditionally have seen gender as being fluid and not fixed or determined by one's biological sex. Many early explorers and ethnographers were aware of these gender variances. This fluidity is noted by Peter Grant in his "The Sauteux Indians[35] about 1804," published in *Les Bourgeois de la Compagnie du Nord-Ouest*. He writes:

I have known several instances of some men who by virtue of some extraordinary dream, had been affected to such a degree as to abandon every custom characteristic of their sex and adopt the dress and manners of a woman. They are never ridiculed or despised by the men on account of their new customs, but on the contrary respected as saints or beings the same degree inspired by the Manitou.[36]

Will Roscoe's chart entitled *Tribal Index of Alternative Gender Roles and Sexuality* indicates that the ethnographer A. Irving Hallowell observed alternative gender roles for both males and females among the Ojibway people in the 1930s and '40s.[37] As well, Ruth Landes observed similar variances in gender roles for women during the same period and writes of these in her books.[38] Contemporary Western society is only beginning to understand what many Aboriginal societies have known since time immemorial. Unlike the ethnographers of the past, who viewed these variations as pathological maladjustments, many Aboriginal societies, including the Anishnaabe, accommodated these variants. Morrisseau's depictions of the nude are a testament to this understanding.

Although attitudes regarding sexuality had been relaxing in the 1980s, the expression of sexuality that deviated from the norm still met with a great deal of opposition. However, in the traditional Anishnaabe world view, gender and sexuality are not defined exclusively in terms of male and female nor, for that matter, in terms of heterosexuality or homosexuality. These dichotomies are Western social constructs in which Aboriginal people were forcibly indoctrinated by institutions such as churches and schools. Gabor Vadas, paraphrasing Morrisseau, stated in an interview for the recent film *A Separate Reality: The Life and Times of Norval Morrisseau*, "Norval sees no reason he should apologize for anything sexual." He continues by stating further, "He made it very clear to me that he is neither gay, straight or bisexual. Everybody could be all of that from Norval's point of view."[39] Gabor's statement not only reveals Morrisseau's rejection of labels, but, I contend, questions the authority and universality of a construct in which sexuality, gender and identity are based on one's biological sex. Morrisseau's view, grounded in an Anishnaabe world view, is extremely important for understanding his erotic artwork. According to anthropologist Sabine Lang, many Native American cultures share a similar world view, which also accepts gender-variant individuals. As Lang writes, they "realize and appreciate transformation, change, and ambiguity in the world at large, as well as individuals."[40]

Within the Ojibway world view there is the concept known as the *agokwa*. This is the Anishnaabe term for the biological male that preformed the gender roles of a woman. (Anthropologists dubbed *agokwa* "berdaches," a term that has recently come under some criticism for being potentially offensive.) Conversely, the term for a biological woman who performs the gender roles of a man is *okitcitakwe* or warrior woman.[41] The *agokwa* was not considered a homosexual because the Anishnaabe did not consider the *agokwa* as being a "deviant" male; they were neither male of female—they belonged to a third gender. As Lang points out, early ethnographers represented the relationships between an *agokwa* and a man as homosexual in their fieldwork because they failed to see that, from an Aboriginal perspective, these relationships involved two people of the same sex but of differing genders. As anthropologist Will Roscoe observes, "Because berdaches were considered members of a distinct gender, native epistemologies classified relationships with them differently."[42] As Sabine Lang writes so succinctly "If you are a man and you have a sexual relationship with a 'berdache,' you are not having sex with another man. You are having sex with a 'berdache.' So the partners of the berdaches technically are never homosexual because they are not having sex with their same gender."[43] Roscoe also adds that, generally, there is a distinction between reproductive and non-reproductive sexual acts, and he writes that non-reproductive sex was valued in its own right and was engaged in for pleasure and emotional rewards; sexual acts were, therefore, not relegated only to the procreative function. However, sexual activity was only a very small part of the *agokwa's* gender role. Among the Ojibway, as among many other tribes, these individuals enjoyed special respect or status within the community because of the role visions or dreams played in determining the *agokwa's* identity. Their identity as *agokwa* was viewed as a result of the divine intervention of other-than-human beings.[44] Anthropologists Callender and Kochems also report that among the Ojibway an *agokwa* was identified by his choice to participate in female activities over male activities.[45]

Historian Bobbalee Ann Shuler has explored differences in interpretation of sexual behaviour between Europeans and traditional Aboriginal people. She writes that in many Aboriginal communities, one's gender classification was not determined on the basis of sexual activity but rather by the person's spirit, character and desire, because the body is recognized as a temporary state and houses the soul-spirit.[46] In a culture in which metamorphosis and the instability of the outer form is so prevalent in the oral traditions, it is evident that the inner reality is, as Southcott has observed, "paramount and the outward appearance is only an incidental attribute of being."[47] This notion is central to understanding Morrisseau's images of sexual intimacy among males.

The image *Indian Erotic Fantasy*, which was included in the Lee-Ann Martin and Morgan Wood exhibition Exposed: the Aesthetics of Aboriginal Art, is one of the images that make visible both the sexual and the spiritual connections between two people (see fig. 4, overleaf). Enclosed within a cocoon, the two male figures exemplify metamorphosis in both a figurative and a literal sense. A number of visual elements underline the interconnections between these beings. Their sexual desire for one another is indicated by their mutual state of arousal, as both figures are depicted with an erection. The background of two shades

Figure 4. INDIAN EROTIC FANTASY

n.d., 152.4 cm × 257.8 cm, Acrylic on canvas, Glenbow
Museum Collection, Calgary, Alberta, 986.226.35.

of blue speaks of both protection and of a spiritual sanction of this relationship.[48] The two nude figures are shown in profile, their bodies outlined with heavy black lines. Although they are represented as two distinct persons, they appear conjoined at the shoulder. Each figure is filled with different opaque colours, indicating the differing racial backgrounds of these individuals. The figure on the left depicts an Aboriginal male against the darker shade of blue, the colour that Morrisseau has explained represents the night sky. From his neck hangs a necklace composed of circles and ovals outlined with a black formline, using the light blue, dark blue, yellow, red and orange to form the design; this same graphic treatment is repeated in the formation of this individual's earlock. He also wears an armband and two wristbands, outlined in the characteristic black formline. These differ from the necklace and earlock in that the shapes are elongated, mimicking an ovoid, while the colours used are a combination of the two shades of blue with the addition of lavender. The second figure is white and non-Aboriginal. Morrisseau employs a number of visual elements to emphasize the interconnection between these two individuals—a connection that is physical, emotional, mental and cognitive. These small black undulating lines are like electric currents passing between these figures, tracing an exchange of energy. It is an image that portrays more than physical attraction as one figure reaches upward to touch the beating heart of the second male figure, who offers no resistance as his own hand is seemly supporting and welcoming the intimate act.

Between the two figures near the bottom of the frame is a series of concentric circles of lavender, turquoise, yellow and red, respectively. These circles are enclosed by a black formline, which also acts as a hub for a number of lines radiating outward and connecting the two figures. Following an ascending line along the posterior of the male figure on the right, the concentric circle pattern repeats with minor variations in both colour and size. The larger of these circles runs parallel to the non-Aboriginal male's calf, buttocks, torso and neck. These larger concentric circles, Martin and Wood inform us, signify the "five stages of life one must pass through in order to free the soul."[49] A series of seven small concentric circles of yellow and blue do not follow a pattern but are randomly placed on the body of the fair-skinned male; on the shaft of his penis, his buttock, wrist, biceps, shoulder and chin. The seventh one differs from the others in that the colour blue has been added, which, along with its placement—in the centre of this male figure's heart—indicates that it is more significant than the others.

In his depiction of the caterpillar, whose body curves around the lovers and physically encases them, Morrisseau creates a narrative rich in symbolism. Its presence speaks of transformation and metamorphosis. In a sense it represents death as a temporary state that evolves into a different state of being. Similarly, the two male figures seem to merge together physically forming a symbiotic existence. Morrisseau's *Indian Erotic Fantasy* visually illustrates a Platonic ideal.

Whether or not Morrisseau was cognizant of Plato's writings on the nature of love, his image expresses the same need for two to meld into one, a notion that has transcended time, as evident in popular culture phenomena from Hallmark cards to Hollywood movies. The title of the image may betray its overall sentiment, because Morrisseau may have used the word "fantasy" to imply an unattainable state.

Very few cultures have defined individuals solely in terms of their sexual orientation or sexual behaviour,[50] and the Anishnaabe are no exception to this—sexual behaviour was a very small part of the *agokwa* role within the Anishnaabe community. The *agokwa* individual took on the role of a woman, and in many instances this also included choosing a same-sexed person as their sexual partner. Morrisseau's erotic depictions call into question the usefulness of what can be defined as the categorically exclusive terms in which identity is delineated. His images question the binary constructs of homosexual and heterosexual even if they do not resolve it. Morrisseau's reluctance to identity himself in terms of these Western constructs not only is a rejection of these labels but also firmly establishes the roots of his identity within an Anishnaabe world view. It is a world view that recognizes and appreciates ambiguity, transformation and the instability of one's outer form.

WHEN TWO WORLDS COLLIDE there is always the possibility that only one world will survive. Fortunately in the body of art I have considered in this discussion, this has not been the outcome. Morrisseau's erotic imagery has left us a legacy that enables us to critique the depiction of the nude and question the social hierarchies embedded in depictions of the nude and sexuality.

Norval Morrisseau's erotic images speak of a different understanding regarding the body, gender and desire. His erotic imagery challenges widespread notions in Western society by putting forward alternatives grounded in an Anishnaabe world view.[51] Western notions regarding the body, gender and sexuality are often touted as expressing the innate nature of human beings; what Morrisseau makes evident is how unstable these notions are. His depictions demonstrate that the authority of the meta-narratives are not absolute, nor are they universal.

NOTES

1 Unfortunately Morrisseau did not document many of his paintings, and no records appear to have been kept with the exception of those by his agents.
2 Anishnaabe, Ojibwa, Ojibway and Chippewa refer to the same group of people. They speak a language that belongs to the Algonquian language family. Ojibway is a common term in Canada, whereas Chippewa is more commonly used in the United States. Anishnaabe is the term the people use to describe themselves.

3 Michel Foucault. *History of Sexuality: An Introduction, vol. 1*. Robert Hurley, trans. New York: Vintage Books, 1990.

4 Foucault, p. 38.

5 Foucault, p. 69.

6 James Clifford quoted in Ann Laura Stoler. *Race and the Education of Desire: Foucault's History of Sexuality and the Colonial Order of Things*. Durham: Duke University Press, 1995: 14.

7 Stoler, p. 4.

8 Morrisseau's adopted son, Gabor Vadas, disclosed this in an interview for the film *A Separate Reality: The Life and Times of Norval Morrisseau*, written and directed by Paul Carvalho for the Canadian Broadcasting Corporation, 2004.

9 Roland Barthes. *Mythologies*. London: Vintage, 1993: 129.

10 Lynda Nead. *The Female Nude: Art, Obscenity and Sexuality*. London: Routledge, 1992: 1.

11 Griselda Pollock. "Screening the Seventies." In *The Feminism and Visual Cultural Reader*. Amelia Jones, ed. London: Routledge, 2003: 81.

12 Nead, p. 23.

13 See Morrisseau's *Legends of My People, the Great Ojibway*. Typed manuscript. Calgary: Glenbow Museum Archives, 1965.

14 Thomas Overholt and J. Baird Callicott. *Clothed-In-Fur and Other Tales: An Introduction to a Ojibwa World View*. Washington, D.C.: University Press of America, 1982: 143.

15 Val Plumwood. *Feminism and the Mastery of Nature*. London: Routledge, 1993: 21.

16 Plumwood, p. 21.

17 Lister Sinclair and Jack Pollock. *The Art of Norval Morrisseau*. Toronto: Methuen, 1979: 125.

18 Mary Beth Southcott. *The Sound of the Drum: The Sacred Art of the Anishnabe*. Erin, ON: Boston Mills Press, 1984: 46. Southcott uses this term to descibe the visual effect she sees in Morriseau's use of black formlines filled with opaque colours, which she considers similar to cloisonné.

19 Southcott, p. 41.

20 John Berger. *Ways of Seeing*. London: BBC/Pelican, 1972: 54.

21 Nead, p. 100.

22 Ruth Landes. *The Ojibwa Woman*. New York: Columbia University Press, 1938: 42.

23 Landes, p. 42.

24 Elizabeth Grosz, "Luce Irigaray and the Ethics of Alterity." In *Sexual Subversions: Three French Feminists*. Sydney: Allen & Unwin, 1989: 179.

25 Nead, p. 47.

26 Kenneth MacKinnon. *Uneasy Pleasures: The Male as Erotic Object*. London: Cygnus Arts of Golden Cockerel Press, 1997: 22.

27 Abigail Solomon-Godeau. *Male Trouble*. London: Thames & Hudson, 1997: 26.

28 Solomon-Godeau, p. 26.

29 Edward Lucie-Smith. *Adam: The Male Figure in Art*. New York: Rizzoli, 1998: 58.

30 Eve Kosofsky Sedgwick. *Epistemology of the Closet*. Berkeley: University of California Press, 1990: 1.

31 For more information see Andrew Stewart's *Art, Desire, and the Body in Ancient Greece*.

32 Lee-Ann Martin. *Exposed: Aesthetics of Aboriginal Erotic Art*. Exhibition catalogue. Regina: MacKenzie Art Gallery, 1999: 43.

33 Basil Johnston. *Ojibway Heritage*. Toronto: McClelland and Stewart, 1990: 5

34 Southcott, p. 80.

35 The Saulteaux, also spelled Sauteux, are a branch of Ojibway and are sometimes referred to as the Plains Ojibway.

36 Peter Grant. "The Sauteux Indians about 1804." In *Les Bourgeois de la Compagnie du Nord-Ouest: Recits de voyages, letters et rapports inedits relatifs au nord-ouest canadien, vol. 2*. L.R. Masson, ed. New York: Antiquarian Press, 1960: 357.

37 Roscoe, p. 237.

38 See Ruth Landes's books *Ojibwa Sociology* and *The Ojibwa Woman* for more information.

39 Quoted in *A Separate Reality*.

40 Sabine Lang. "Various Kinds of Two-Spirit People: Gender Variance and Homosexuality in Native American Communities." In *Two-Spirit People: Native American Gender Identity, Sexuality, and Spirituality*. Champaign, IL: University of Illinois Press, 1997: 114.

41 Will Roscoe. *The Changing Ones: Third and Fourth Genders in Native North America*. New York: St. Martin's Press, 1998: 214, 237.

42 Roscoe, p. 10.

43 Lang, p. 205.

44 Roscoe, p. 14.

45 Charles Callender and Lee M. Kochems. "The North American Berdache." *Current Anthropology*. Vol. 24, No. 4 (Aug–Sept 1998): 452.

46 Bobbalee Ann Shuler. *More Sin than Pleasure: A Study in Cultural Conflict*. PhD dissertation, University of Wyoming, 1994: 33.

47 Southcott, p. 38.

48 In an interview with Métis historian Olive Dickson, Morrisseau shares with her the meaning of these two colours and the circumstances in which he was given these colours.

49 Martin and Wood, p. 41.

50 For more information on other non-Western cultures see Dominique Fernandez, *A Hidden Love: Art and Homosexuality*, pp. 158–181, or James Smalls, *Homosexuality in Art*, Chapter 4.

51 Barthes, p. 129.

FEAR OF A
CHANGELING MOON

A Rather Queer Tale
from a Cherokee Hillbilly

Daniel Heath Justice

Ｔ HIS IS AN old Cherokee story about the Moon and why he
hides his face. *He is marked by shame from a time, long ago,
when he visited his sister, the Sun, in darkness and lay with her in
forbidden ways. Unaware of her secret lover's identity, and fascinated
by the pleasures she found after dark, the Sun enjoyed herself for quite
some time, but eventually her curiosity got the better of her. So, after
one particularly wild night, and when her visitor was spent and asleep,
she pulled a brand from the fire and brought it to her pallet, only to
find that the dream lover was none other than her own brother. He
awoke at her cry of recognition and, seeing the horror in her eyes and
knowing the ancient laws against incest, fled into the darkness. Now
he rarely shows his face to the world, and even less often to his sister in
the daytime sky. He wears his shame on his face, and he is alone.*

I'VE BEEN IN Canada for five years now, going on six, and I'm
still finding it a fascinating country. Its differences from the U.S.,
where I was born and raised, are stark in so many ways, not the

least being a rather civilized approach towards sex and sexuality. It's a welcome change. I grew up in the Colorado Rockies, although my home for the five years before moving to Canada was Lincoln, Nebraska, firmly in the heart of repressive Republicanism. The year before I left Lincoln saw the passage of the so-called Defence of Marriage Act, an amendment to the state constitution banning not only same-sex marriage but also domestic partnerships, state-funded insurance for same-sex couples and any other state recognition of happy queer coupledom. The act, specifically known as Amendment 416, passed with about 70 per cent approval from the electorate. Not a particularly supportive environment in which to explore the possibilities of bodily pleasure, especially for those whose desires moved beyond the bounds of heterosexual coupling.

Although a puritanical undercurrent is constantly buckling the earth beneath U.S. politics and social interaction, I was quite fortunate during my formative years, as my parents have always been rather liberated on matters of sex. They married when my dad was thirty-nine, my mom eighteen; he'd been married three times, had three kids and was well acquainted with the pleasures of the flesh. My mom, though a virgin when they met, was a no-nonsense mountain woman who knew what felt good and wasn't shy about letting Dad know it. As a child and teenager, I often surreptitiously climbed the floor-to-ceiling bookshelves in the living room and took down Dad's latest porn movie rentals, and they gave me an eye-opening education that demystified many things that men and women (or women and women, given straight porn's predilection for gratuitous lesbian action) did together. Still, the sloppy wet sex films and my parents' generally open attitude towards sex didn't reveal all sexual secrets. There were other realms of pleasure that were outside of my experience, but they weren't beyond my desire. I had a hunger I couldn't name for a very long time, but it stalked my dreams.

My earliest dreams were about werewolves, and they were terrible. Thick, rancid fur, gleaming fangs and glowing eyes, hot breath and bloodied claws crept through my dreams with ghoulish persistence, forcing me into sweat-choked wakefulness every few months for most of my young life. They often accompanied the fattening moon, which was a complicated mystery in my mind: an alien beauty that beckoned softly to me with his brilliance, and a capricious being whose presence inspired the transformation of ordinary mortals into murderous canine shapeshifters. I rarely ventured from my house during these monthly visits. If by some great misfortune I had to expose myself to such a night, my heart would clench painfully in my throat, my ears and eyes would strain for the slightest hint of shadowed shapes in the darkness just beyond the limits of my senses and my legs would shudder with the prescience of desperate prey, just moments before I'd run, tears in my eyes, as fast as my little legs would carry me to safety. As I grew older the observable signs of the terror lessened, but only through great effort and the repetitious affirmation, "Don't be stupid. There's nothing there." *Nothing there.*

There's nothing quite like the fat-faced moon pulling himself slowly, gently over jagged peaks on a clear Colorado night. The moonlight flows across valleys and cliffs, a liquid mirror transforming a once-familiar landscape into a strange faerie-realm. The closest things to wolves in my district are coyotes and mongrel dogs—hardly the symbolic harbingers of ravenous, insatiable hunger. But reasoned and romantic arguments—even appeals to the aesthetic beauty of a Rocky Mountain midnight—faded before the fear that rose round and diminished with the moon every month. *Nothing there.*

When I was three, I learned that my dad was "an Indian." The knowledge horrified me. Indians, as I'd already learned well from Bugs Bunny cartoons and Saturday afternoon television matinees, were treacherous, big-nosed and beady-eyed redskin ravagers of the prairies. They were ugly, stupid, gauche and—worst of all to the school nerd who turned to books for sanctuary—"uncivilized." Only the Great Plains chiefs, with their flamboyant feathered headdresses and beaded buckskins, were at all appealing, but even they ended up dead or fading away into the white man's sunset, muttering in monosyllables all the way.

I wasn't like them. My skin was light, my hair thin and sandy brown, like Mom's. Even Dad, although dark skinned, didn't look or act like those Indians. Instead of hanging in braids, his hair was buzz-cut close to his head. He wore flannels, not buckskins, and had never, as far as I knew, raided a stagecoach or covered wagon. Ours was the life of a working-class mining family in the Colorado Rockies, and whatever difference our Indigenous heritage made—the Cherokee and Shawnee Spears, Justices and Foremans on Dad's side, the Cherokee or possibly Chickasaw Fays and Sparkses on Mom's—was something I didn't want to think about or dwell on. The alienation Dad felt as one of the two visibly Indian people in the district wasn't a concern to me, nor was Mom's growing awareness of my self-distancing from home and heritage. Nothing about my people was interesting to me—not Wilma Mankiller, nor Sequoyah, Nancy Ward/ Nanyehi, John Ross, Stand Watie, Ada-gal'kala/Little Carpenter, Will Rogers, Emmet Starr or the rest. Not our history, our cultural legacies, our philosophies and world views, our ancient and current homelands. And certainly not the darkness that stalked the Cherokees: allotment, missionaries, relocation and the Trail of Tears, the Cherokee death march that still haunts my family and our history. Everything about Indians was tragic to my mind, and I'd had enough of tragedy.

I wanted to be something different. Beauty always beckoned to me, and I pursued it with single-minded desperation. At age five or six, I discovered Wonder Woman. Lynda Carter as the Amazing Amazon was a figure right out of the heavens. Not only was she beautiful—with dark brown hair, golden skin and a colourful costume—but she could also kick ass and champion peace and justice at the same time. She was beauty incarnate. Between her, Dolly Parton and Crystal Gayle, I was hooked. They shared a beauty of excess, of gilt and glitter, spangles, rhinestones and sequins. Wonder Woman was superhuman and dedicated to good; Dolly was comfortable with her oversized boobs and her flashy flamboyance, and Crystal's sensuality and floor-length hair capped the appeal of her melodic voice and down-home country kindness.

But my male peers didn't share my attraction to these women. The only thing they remarked on about Lynda Carter and Dolly were how big their "titties" were, and Crystal didn't even register on their radar. These attitudes were blasphemy to my budding country diva sensibilities, of course, which further alienated me from boys my age. These women weren't sex objects—they were figures to venerate, adore and imitate. I wanted long hair like Crystal's, outfits like Dolly's and the ability to change into a sexy superhero just by spinning around wildly for a few minutes. (I made myself deathly ill two or three times a week by trying just that.) Nothing seemed to bother these women—not poverty, mockery, misogyny or even being captured by Nazi supervillains—and I wanted nothing less than to share some of that campy glamour.

On those rare occasions some of my male classmates would ask me to play with them, I'd invariably demand to be the token female of the bunch: if we were playing G.I. Joe, I was the Baroness or Scarlett; if it was Super Friends, I was Wonder Woman or Batgirl; Ozma or Dorothy of Oz; and then, when Masters of the Universe came along, I was enthralled, as I had three beautiful and scantily clad superwomen to emulate—Teela, the Sorceress, Evil-Lyn—and two of them had iron brassieres and bracers, just like Wonder Woman.

THIS QUIRK OF mine didn't go unnoticed by the other boys. If I wasn't outright mocked, I was soon completely excluded from play. It unnerved them to have one of their own so enthusiastically leaping around the playground shouting, "Wisdom of Athena, Beauty of Aphrodite—*I am Wonder Woman!*" So I'd return to the girls, who always seemed to enjoy my company, especially the oddballs who didn't have a place among the more popular and conventionally pretty of the feminine persuasion. Cyndi was one such friend; she lived just a few blocks away. Cyndi didn't mind if I was Daisy Duke one day or Wicket the Ewok or Smurfette the next, and she liked to have a friend, boy or not, to play with. We accepted each other, shared our secrets and pains and struggled to survive the teasing and abuse lobbed on us by the others.

The realm of the fantastic was a safe place for the weird kids like me. A fluid understanding of gender and identity, together with a love of the myths, fairy tales and legends of faraway places and peoples combined to create imaginative possibilities far beyond the realities of the fading little mining town I called home. My predilection for the strange and fey didn't go unnoticed by my peers, although the response was hardly what I wanted it to be. By fourth grade I'd been renamed various times and with increasing scorn: "fairy" was quite common, as was "sissy." "Queer" and "faggot" made their way into my consciousness during this time, but the epithet of choice wielded against me was "Tinkerbell." I hated it; still do. It was bad enough to be called that by kids my own age, but in my K-12 school the name travelled quickly, and the worst of it was, as a ten-year-old, to be called Tinkerbell by juniors and seniors in high school.

There was just so much abuse I could handle, so by that time I'd given up most of the gender play and dolls, but I was still drawn to the theatrical, the elaborate and the ornate, and those things deemed feminine and womanly (and thus supposedly inferior) but that I saw as lovely beyond words. So, as the resident artist, actor and all-around aesthetic eccentric—thus "faggot"—I retained the title of Tinkerbell among some of the school Neanderthals until graduation, a title I'd have gratefully surrendered had I been given the choice.

I had other names, too, but these were given with love and affection. The one I preferred was Booner, after the great white frontiersman and (although my parents didn't know it at the time they gave me the name) celebrated Cherokee killer, Daniel Boone. It's the name I'm still known by when I go home. (My partner was much amused on a recent trip to find the name slightly changed now, though, when we walked into one of the local gift shops and a woman I worked with as a teenager paused in her phone conversation because she had to say hi to "Doctor Booner.") I've never much minded that name, because I always liked having a moniker that was unique to me. And it fit my interests in fantasy and exotica, especially when I learned that a troll on the Shetland Islands was once known as "the Booner." But the names given by kids in school were a different matter entirely.

People who look back on school interaction in childhood as a time of peace, idealism and happiness are either liars, incredibly lucky or among the masses who enjoyed tormenting the rest of us during adolescence. And those who say that kids aren't reflective enough to know what they're doing are fools; it's easy to say that when not on the receiving end of a bully's words or fists. My parents and home life were wonderful—there was never a time I felt unloved or unaccepted as a human being—but they couldn't protect me from every bit of cruelty I dealt with at school, where each act of misnaming, combined with the isolation of difference, worked to chisel away at the world I'd created for myself, a place I could escape to without fear of rejection or abuse.

The worlds I wanted to go to were Faerie, the marvellous land of Oz, Krynn, Middle-earth—all the places where freaks and misfits fled to be heroes and magicians, where their essence and integrity were more important than who they failed to be, couldn't be . . . or refused to be. I wouldn't be a Cherokee kid with delusions of European grandeur or a misfit nerd who desperately wanted to be popular but couldn't surrender to the demands of conformity. And I wouldn't be a boy unsure about his masculinity, a boy for whom beauty and gentility meant more than muscle and meanness. When I'd walk with my dogs through pine and aspen woods, I'd fantasize about walking unaware through the veil between our world and that of the Fair Folk, never to return to the pain of adolescence again. There was certainly shadow in Faerie—the dark side of the moon—but it belonged here and, if treated with respect, took no notice of intruders. Even werewolves could be mastered in Faerie.

MOST OF THE DREAMS I can remember from my youth were nightmares. But there was one recurring vision that would visit a couple times a year that didn't carry the terror of the others. *I dreamed of a deep forest, thick with foreign trees and plants: gnarled oaks, choking underbrush, sumac and ivy, birches and maples, mushrooms, mosses and deep, dark pools of cold, mountain-fed waters. There was shadow here, but I was safe from a crouching menace that kept others far away but that whispered softly to me. I'd walk through this woodland in my dream, drawn by a force that lurked within the fear and frustration of an unknown world, leading me farther into the dark recesses of the ancient trees, past skittish deer and rabbits, over moss-heavy boulders strewn through the undergrowth like forgotten toys in a sandbox. I knew the destination long before I saw it. And although I felt fear, I also knew beyond doubt that I was going home.*

As I retrace the steps of this dream, it fades and shimmers in my memory like a parched man's mirage—I want to hold it, to taste it, but it slips away to reappear elsewhere, just out of my reach. I walk in eternal twilight, fearful that I might never see daylight again in this dark, oppressive, labyrinthine forest. Nothing there. *And before the*

thought is fully formed, I see the light, a ray of gilded sunshine break-
ing through the canopy to fall softly in scattered shafts across a small
cottage hidden deeply in the trees. The house is small and dark, and
the shutters are tightly drawn. Nothing moves or makes a sound—no
birdsong, no mice rustling in last year's crackling leaves, no breeze to
tousle my hair. Only a thin trail of smoke, which creeps slowly from
the chimney. It is the house that has been calling to me, calls me still,
and each time I stop at the edge of the clearing, just within the woods,
afraid to go farther, certain only that I am home.

My pubescent transformations were not welcomed with
enthusiasm, at least by me. One afternoon, when I was about
fourteen, my mom and I were sitting on the couch when she suddenly reached over and pushed my chin up. "Well, son," she said
with a proud grin, "I think it's time your dad showed you how to
shave." I burst into tears, shocking both my parents, who had no
idea why I was so horrified at the prospect of growing facial hair.

Facial hair belonged to the brute, the beast. I fancied myself
more elegant, more refined. *Elves don't grow beards.* That much,
at least, I knew from my reading. Facial hair was a sign of mor-
tality, of humanity, and I'd long harboured the secret fantasy
that maybe I was an elfin changeling or fairy prince left by mistake or circumstance to live among humans, until such time as
my people were ready to claim me. But the revelations of puberty
destroyed even that furtive fantasy.

Body hair and genital changes weren't so bad; they were actually quite intriguing. But the developing beard, the underarm
sweat and necessity of deodorant, the cracking voice, the nose
that grew out of proportion to the rest of my face, the feet that
grew so quickly that more than once I put a hole in the drywall
from tripping up the stairs—all these events combined to remind
me over and over that I was just another awkward, dorky kid
who'd never be the noble prince. And besides that, I was also an
Indian, and everyone knew that although there were supposedly

plenty of Cherokee princesses running around, there weren't any Cherokee *princes*. Puberty changed me in more ways than I anticipated, and it was a transformation that didn't begin or end with the phases of the moon.

When I was a senior in high school, a female friend showed me a *Blueboy* magazine that her aunt had given her; they both knew it was a gay men's magazine, but they were still thrilled with the beauty of the men within. I was stunned by the pictures. I'd seen more than my fair share of porn, from pirated *Playboys* to those many movies Dad kept on the top shelf of the living room bookshelf. But I'd never seen anything like the men in this magazine, nor read anything like the erotic stories inside. An awareness began to edge its way into my consciousness, and I borrowed the magazine for a week, after having made up some lame and likely entirely transparent reason for wanting it.

I'd been called a faggot and queer all my life, but I always believed that I wasn't gay, as the guys I knew held no attraction to me whatsoever. Most guys my age were crude, cruel and unpleasant, or simply unattractive, uninteresting or distant. I avoided circumstances of intimacy with other guys, even getting a special dispensation in high school that kept me out of the locker room so that I wouldn't have to change in front of others. If I was gay, I reasoned, surely I'd have to be lusting after every man I saw. But the men in the *Blueboy* were wholly different than the ones I knew: enthusiastically sexual, bold and comfortable with themselves and beautiful beyond words. These men weren't "faggots"—they were *gods.* It was the first realization that my personality, all my quaint and curious traits and habits, weren't the problem; the problem rested in those who were so very blind to this beauty.

BUT FEAR AND SHAME kept me from fully understanding this lesson, and although I bought gay porn from that point on—either through the mail or during fearful live bookstore purchases—I explained it away. *I'm not gay*, I'd whisper to myself as I'd ogle the pictures with unrestrained desire. *I just can't watch straight porn; after all, most women involved with straight porn are in it against their will. At least gay men are willing participants. I won't be party to the subjugation of women.* It was desperate self-delusion, and it worked for years.

I dated a lovely woman for nine months my sophomore year in university—we never kissed or groped, and I broke up with her partially because she wanted to have sex. Then, two years later, I lost my virginity at age twenty-one, to a sweet woman I felt no love or real affection for, having grown tired of people questioning my masculinity and sexuality. After I came, I rushed to the bathroom and retched, dry heaves tearing through my throat and stomach, disgusted at myself and at a betrayal I didn't fully understand. I still fought the dream of the woodland cottage.

THE MOST VIVID DREAM I ever had, though, was, of course, about werewolves.

It's a dark summer night, with only streetlights to guide my way as I walk through town. The houses are quiet, the people asleep, or worse; no dogs bark, no owl calls echo across the mountains, no bats whir breathlessly in the fluorescent light seeking miller moths and other juicy night-fliers. I walk alone, a fifteen-year-old kid in a silent mining town, heading towards an unseen destination, and then I stop in the white glow of a streetlight. My eyes scan the distance, peering through darkness to a house that seems to be writing *under the next light just a block away.*

I walk towards the house, which pulsates in the shadows with an irregular rhythm, the ragged heartbeat of a crippled bird. I'm not sure what's happening until I reach the middle of the block and see that the house is covered with hundreds of werewolves. They crawl over one another, snarling and growling low, slipping greasily across the hairy forms of their kindred, fucking and biting and humping and feasting on the remnants of the house's inhabitants, or each other. It's a horrific sight, and they don't know I'm there, but I can't move, I can't scream. I can't go anywhere, even though my house is only two short blocks away in the opposite direction. All I can do is watch in terri-fied fascination as the werewolves, bound by instinct and desire I can't imagine—at least not in my waking life—engage in every debauched, disgusting act imaginable around the saliva- and cum- and blood-stained house beneath them.

Then I hear a low chorus of growls behind me, and I know before turning that there are scores of the creatures crouched in the road, in the streetlight, behind me. Some sit softly and watch me, hunger and hatred burning in their green eyes. Others fuck in orgiastic abandon, but they watch me, too, even as sweat-slick furry haunches pump slop-pily together. I'm alone under their collective gaze. My first fear is the obvious one, that they'll swarm and tear me apart. But they sit there, waiting and watching, and then I realize why they wait as the clouds drift away from the moon and my skin begins to burn. The flesh gets tight, like a T-shirt that's suddenly too small, and it darkens as thick hair bristles under the surface. They think I'm one of them, *my mind screams,* but I'm not; I never will be. *They move forward in hissing welcome, and I run blindly towards a nearby alley, blind to everything but the necessity to get away from them, to get away from the moon and the changes he summons.* Nothing there. *Behind me in the darkness rise the savage sounds of gleeful pursuit, and I am the hunted—I am prey.*

The breakdown came when I was twenty. I'd tried to be a good Presbyterian, Episcopalian, New Ager and pseudo-Eastern Orthodox Christian, but truth eluded me in those stone walls and narrow doctrines. I'd discovered that my mentor, a man whose Eurocentric pretence and self-delusion were even more compul-sive than my own, had a questionable reputation regarding his relationships with artistic and slender young men. People in my department called me his "boy toy." The beauty I'd been seeking in falsehood was a corrosive poison to the spirit; if I hadn't reached back and taken hold of my family then, in those fragile weeks, I probably wouldn't have survived until summer. But I heard them whisper to me at night, family met and unknown, spirits calling me back to home and the mountains. At last, I answered.

When I called Mom and told her that I wanted to come home, she was very quiet, then said, "I'm so glad to hear that you're not ashamed of where you come from anymore." I hung up the phone and wept. I'd never meant for my parents to believe that I was rejecting *them*: I was rejecting my peers, our poverty, the mindset of the mountains, ignorance and bigotry and despair. But how could they think anything else? They'd watched me run away so desperately, cut myself away so ruthlessly, and still they never turned away from me.

The identity I'd constructed was being stripped away, and it was an agonizing process. But there was no real choice. It was either truth with all its pain, or death in deception. I could no longer deny my family, my people—Justice, Fay, Spears, Schryver, Bandy, Sparks and Foreman. Cherokee, Shawnee, German Jew, French and mongrel Celt, maybe even Chickasaw. A light-skinned mixed-blood *Ani-yunwiya*, one of the Real Human Beings. *Tsalagi*—Cherokee, the people of caves and another speech, the people of the mountains, the people who survived the bloody Trail and who thrive in spite of the heartbreak and horror of manifest murder. We are of the Cherokee Nation, and although we were of the allotment diaspora, we are Cherokees still. There is no more shame in surviving. The shame isn't ours. The elders teach of balance, of the necessity of right actions, of truth. My parents raised me to be honest with myself and others and to seek those who think the same.

We name ourselves now.

It seemed that I'd finally exorcised the restless spirits of my childhood and adolescence. I'd returned my spirit to the mountains, dedicated myself to reclaiming a history and those traditions two generations removed from me and my parents. To all conventional appearances I was well adjusted. No flamboyance, no cross-dressing, no dolls. But the night sweats continued, albeit on a lesser scale, as did the dreams of pursuit and horror. There weren't any more thick-furred fiends hunting me through the streets of my hometown, but I'd often dream of wolfsong, howls in the deep recesses of my dreams, reminders of a darker time and of unfinished business. *Nothing there.*

The dream house returned as well, and with more frequency. And the peril I'd felt as the dream werewolves watched me and waited had now descended on the house, now a place fully alive with menace. The house in the forest, a dark place filled with deeper shadows, wanted me—it whispered to me and called itself *home.*

When I was twenty-three, the doors of the cottage opened to me, and I stepped across its weathered threshold into a welcoming darkness. In the two years since I'd left Colorado to go to graduate school in Nebraska, I'd gradually come to a partial realization about the desires that moved me, feelings and understandings that were as much a part of me as my Cherokee heritage and mountain upbringing. At an academic conference in St. Louis, Missouri, as my hands slid across the pale skin of a fun and quirky man from Michigan, his lips and tongue gently teasing my own, the cottage surrendered its secret. Then I surrendered my fear. That night, when he held me tightly against his sweaty body, our desire a blissful weight on our entwined forms, the hunger I'd always known but never named was finally sated. The beauty I'd sought had awakened within me, within that long-suffering flesh that I'd always treated with the suspicion of treachery. The Moon's shame was not mine; his shame was dishonesty and deception, not desire. He abused the trust of his sister, the Sun, and it's this violation that marks him. My passion was something wholly different. As I lay naked in the arms of that hungry man, the darkness dissipated in silver moonlight and the house faded into memory. I knew, at last, that I wasn't alone.

And I've never had a werewolf dream since.

· I came out in my second year of graduate school at the University of Nebraska-Lincoln. One of the first gay friends I made was a tall, gorgeous blond named Billy.* Gentle, kind and thoughtful—oh, how I lusted after him! It was a lust unrequited—or, at least, unfulfilled—but it was a rewarding friendship while it lasted. He and his boyfriend, Tyrell* (my lust for whom *was* requited when their relationship was on hiatus, but that's a rather sordid story that I'm not particularly proud of), introduced me to the gay culture of Lincoln, and to the better of the city's two gay bars: the Q. I've never been much of a fan of the bar culture, but the Q was the one place to go where the music was good and the dancing was fun, and where hot men enjoyed one another's company without shame or fear and passionate women found mutual desire on the dance floor.

One evening, Billy and I decided to go to the Q and hang out for a while. When we got there, we discovered that there was a drag show planned for the night. So, both being in a rather mellow mood, we ordered drinks and sat by the stage, chatting between acts.

About an hour into the evening's entertainment, a dance-mix song began to throb from the speakers. I couldn't place the tune, but it sounded vaguely familiar. About that time, Billy—who faced the stage—let out a gasp of horror. I turned to watch one of the homeliest drag performers I'd ever seen slink out onto the stage, dressed from head to toe as Disney's Pocahontas. At that moment, I recognized the song as "Colors of the Wind" from the cartoon's soundtrack. I sat there in stunned silence as the queen began to jump up and down, singing an old-time

---

* *The names of people in this essay have been changed.*

Hollywood war whoop, channelling the spirits of all the savage squaws in bad TV Westerns.

And then, from the audience, came the all-too-familiar sound of "whoo-whoo-whoo," as men throughout the room began to slap their hands to their open mouths and laugh uproariously at the white drag queen in redface on the stage.

The Q should have been a safe place that night, and it was—for racist white people. But not for us. Billy and I left very soon after the Pocahontas performance was finished. He went home to Tyrell, and I went home to take a shower, suddenly feeling very sick and very unclean. It was one of my last visits to the Q.

In all the time I've been in Toronto, I've never once been to a gay bar. I like thinking of this city as a place removed from such experiences, that the anti-Aboriginal racism that permeates Canadian politics, media and mainstream opinion wouldn't make its way to a queer club if my partner and I decide to go dancing one night, or if a friend and I just want to sit at a table and talk. I like to think that I could just enjoy myself in a place where queerness is the norm, where I wouldn't have to be assaulted by another drag queen in a corset playing Indian to a bunch of jeering white folks.

And if I'm wrong, which I probably am, I'd rather not know it.

THE FIRST GRADUATE course I ever taught was burdened with the rather awkward title of "First Nations Literatures: Lesbian, Gay, Bisexual, Transgendered, and Two-Spirited Native Writers." There were eight students, all non-Native—six ostensibly straight women, one queer woman and one gay man—and we studied works by openly queer writers from both sides of the border, such as Chrystos, Tomson Highway, Greg Sarris, Craig Womack, Joy Harjo, Gregory Scofield and Beth Brant. It was a powerful experience. The male student, when presenting on Womack's coming out/coming-of-age novel *Drowning in Fire*, began to sob uncontrollably as he talked about one passage of the novel, where the protagonist, Josh Henneha, looks out over an expanse of water at sunset and comes to a point of acceptance of himself and his desires. The student found release in that scene of the book, words that named something of his own struggle to name and embrace his sexuality—and all the fears, hopes, pleasures and sacrifices that such acceptance necessitates.

Such moments are all too rare in teaching, and they're a gift when they arrive. Yet not all the course was as powerful. A student mentioned how interesting it was that although we were reading all these amazing texts by queer Native writers, we never actually talked about *sex*. I was taken aback by the statement, but not because it was inaccurate. What shocked me was that, in a city with a thriving queer community and a country with some of the most progressive attitudes towards sexuality in the hemisphere, we'd gone half the term reading books that had some of the most eloquent, profoundly moving scenes of sexuality and physical pleasure in contemporary literature, and yet we'd never discussed these scenes. We'd never said fun, festive and troubling words from the texts like *fuck*, *suck*, *cunt* or *cock*, or even used the rather more clinical *vagina* or *penis*.

In short, we'd never dealt with one of the substantive issues the literature itself was expressing. For these writers, embracing their desire for others of the same gender wasn't something separate from—but was fundamentally a part of—their struggle to express their dignity as Native people. Just as indigenousness itself has long been a colonialist target, so too has our joy, our desire, our sense of ourselves as beings able to both give and receive pleasure. To take joy in sex isn't just about enjoying the bump and grind, suck and squirt, lick and quiver of hot moist flesh on flesh. It's about being beautiful to ourselves and others. And such loving self-awareness is a hard thing to come by in a world that sees Aboriginal peoples as historical artifacts, degraded vagrants or grieving ghosts. To take joy in our bodies—and those bodies in relation to others—is to strike out against five-hundred-plus years of disregard, disrespect and dismissal.

So, we talked about it in class, even when it was difficult. We spoke about the things we hadn't discussed until that point. I addressed my own discomfort in talking about sexual matters in the classroom, a stand-offishness that I'd developed as an openly gay teaching assistant in a homophobic state, where just being out was a political act with the very real danger of aggressive reaction by students. Some of the straight students talked about finding an unfamiliar beauty in the works they'd read and were far more comfortable with reading across that experiential gap than I'd anticipated. The queer students found something of themselves in these writers' work but in a way that acknowledged both connections and differences without collapsing the two together.

And I was reminded again that I wasn't in Nebraska anymore. In Canada, as a gay man, I wasn't a second-class citizen. (As a Native man, however, the jury is still out. But I digress . . .) And queer sexuality, although not treated with universal acceptance, isn't a realm of inquiry alienated from the critical work of the academy. Teaching about sex and sexuality was both a liberating experience and a frightening jump into the realm of some of the most emotionally reactive social fears, phobias and dysfunctions. Friends who have taught queer lit courses in the U.S. have encountered blistering criticism from aggressively politicized students (and, sometimes, administrators) who believe that there's nothing worthwhile to be learned from talking about sex, especially sex and desire they consider deviant because of the archaic admonitions of an arrogant and hostile god with cosmic delusions of grandeur.

I was fearful of this reaction but was both surprised and pleased to discover no such anti-intellectualism among these students in this place. There's a broader public consciousness in Canada, and it's one of the reasons why I will never return to the U.S. to live. This is home for me now. It's not a perfect country, by any means, but to my admittedly limited experience it's a place where difference doesn't demand attack; you can ask questions, even difficult ones, and anticipate a respectful response, even from those who disagree. The two-spirit lit class, although small, was mixed in political orientation, background, comfort level, but all involved were committed to the intellectual questions elicited by our readings. We differed on a number of points and discussed our disagreements, coming away with a stronger sense of what was at stake in sex. I've been thankful that this attitude towards discussing sexuality has been the case with all of my classes and the vast majority of my students since that time. It's not a constant point of discussion, but we don't ignore or minimize it when the issue emerges from course readings. When the atmosphere is one of committed intellectual analysis of texts and their ideas, with mutually respectful interaction with one another, *everyone* has a place in the conversation, and whether conservative or progressive, queer or straight, avowedly religious or affirmatively agnostic or atheist, we can all learn something from the willingness to engage some of these basic questions of life, love and belonging. Because, like it or not, we share a world as well as a classroom, and if we can't talk about the larger implications of sex in the intellectual arena of the academy—implications both positive and negative—we can hardly expect to deal with them in any thoughtful way in the larger public and political sphere.

The discussion in class that day was a good one, and it opened my eyes to some of my own fears and repressions. And I've thought a lot about it since. Queer desire is a reality of life for hundreds of millions of people the world over, and the expression of that desire is an intimate fuel for the cause of liberation among many dominated and oppressed peoples. As a scholar, and as a

queer Native man, I have responsibilities to truth—both cere-
bral and bodily—and to understand how those truths can serve
our dignity and survival in respectful, affirming and construc-
tive ways. To ignore sex and embodied pleasure in the cause of
Indigenous liberation is to ignore one of our greatest resources.
It is to deny us one of our most precious gifts.

Every orgasm can be an act of decolonization.

I CAME TO CANADA almost six years ago, and a lot has changed
in that time. The boyfriend I came here with became my husband, then my ex, as his own desires took him elsewhere. I've
met a lot of wonderful people, including a number of fabulous and well-adjusted two-spirit folks who find strength in
the knowledge that we weren't always perceived as strange,
deviant or disposable. In the traditions of many Indigenous
nations, queer folks had—and continue to have—special gifts
granted by the Creator for the benefit of our families and the
world at large. In this understanding, our sexuality isn't just a
part of our Nativeness—it's fuel for the healing of our nations.
And although my own nation isn't quite as progressive in this
regard—being predominantly Southern Baptist, the Cherokee
Nation in Oklahoma has the dubious and sadly retrograde distinction of being one of (if not *the*) first Native nation to pass
a same-sex marriage ban—the fact that there's still significant
debate in the Nation on this issue gives me hope for the future. It
may take us a while to come around, but it'll happen. The sacred
fire doesn't burn only for straight folks. We queer folks dance
around the fire, too, our voices strong, our hearts full, our spirits shining. We have gifts of healing to bring, too.

Rollie Lynn Riggs was a queer mixed-blood Cherokee, a
poet and a playwright. His play *Green Grow the Lilacs* became
the musical *Oklahoma!* and is still regarded as one of the finest
studies of the mindset of the people of that state. It's also devoid

of Indians. Their absence is palpable, a visible erasure from a man who proudly claimed his Cherokee heritage but left the land of his people because of his sexuality. Oklahoma lingered in his mind, wandering through the red dusk of his imagination until he died of cancer in a New York City hospital. Throughout his life he explored in the shadows what it was to be Indian and gay in a world that had no use for either. And he died alone.

Riggs and I share much in our love of language, our connection to the land and the people and our struggles with understanding our desires. But his rich and artistically inspiring life is also an object lesson in the corrosive consequences of accepting the world's bigotry as a measure of your own worth. He's a much-honoured queer Cherokee forefather, but I don't want to be like him. I want to continue to live the life and celebrate the love he couldn't. And if the spirits are willing, I will.

It's been over eleven years now since I began the long walk back to Cherokee pride and wholeness, and about nine since I came out. I'm now with a beautiful, blue-eyed, big-hearted Scots-Canadian man who has taught me more about love, passion and tenderness than I'd ever thought to know in all the years of self-hatred and shame that came before. In his gentle eyes I am lovely and desired, not for what I can give to him alone but for what we can give one another. It helps that he's also more than happy to help me make a horizontal stand against colonization whenever I'm in the mood—and, being the committed and passionate activist that I am, I am often in the mood.

I think back on this continuing journey, all the unexpected twists and double-backs along the trail, where fragile flesh has hungered for human touch and all too often came away unfulfilled. Would awkward and insecure eighteen-year-old Booner recognize the relatively confident and self-assured thirty-two-year-old Daniel? In those days I thought I'd be a perfectly "civilized," tweed-bound Oxford don and High Church Christian apologist by this point, not a balding, goateed Cherokee nationalist and proud son of the Rockies with multiple tattoos and piercings, a queer Native lit professor living and loving in the semi-socialist wilds of Canada. Booner had expected to have a wife and children, although he had no physical desire for women, nor any significant need to be a father. Although he had furtive dreams of sex with men, he certainly never imagined finding a deep and abiding love with a same-sex partner. Would that shy, scared and ashamed young man have faced all the mingled fears of the flesh earlier if he'd have known that surrendering to the wolfsong and the moonlit shadows of the night would have brought such a healing balm to the spirit of his older self?

I'm not at all sure that he'd have understood or approved if he could see the man who would one day type these words. But maybe, when walking his dogs on a cold, clear winter's night, as he stood looking to the lonely moon's scarred face in the Colorado darkness, he might have known that his hunger was anything but a curse, that his desire was fundamentally different from that of the shame-marked Moon, that the howls in the dark dreams were a kinship cry drawing him towards all the primal power and beauty that passion could offer. Wolves aren't monsters; the monsters abide in deception, fear and self-loathing, not in truthful joy. We all hunger; we long to be loved and to love in return. That, at least, he might have found comforting as he trudged through the moonlit snow towards the warming lights of home.

RED HOT
TO THE TOUCH

WRi[gh]ting

Indigenous Erotica

Kateri Akiwenzie-Damm

*I*T WAS JUST *that she wanted to touch him. That's what started it. He had such soft-looking skin, she longed to run her hands over him, rub the back of his hand over her face, like she did with silk scarves or buckskin gloves. He was standing in front of her, telling her about gaits, how to mix the plaster, about backtracking and how animals sniff the air to follow a scent, and she'd have to put her hands behind her back to keep from reaching for him. Just one touch is all she wanted.*

At the time I first started thinking about erotica and began to realize how difficult it was to find erotica by Indigenous writers, residential school abuse was becoming a huge issue across the country. A lot of people came forward publicly for the first time with their stories and for the first time I heard about and began to understand what the term "intergenerational impacts" meant to us as First Nations people. I grieved about the violence and pain and lovelessness that had been forced into our communities—but

I also knew that we were so much more, that despite being victimized, we were not victims, that someone else's violence and hatred could never fully define us. I grieved for violated innocence but longed for wholeness and joy.

They often talked for hours. He laughed and sang to her. She rhymed off naughty limericks and ranted about this and that colonizing government.

"Don't get me started," she'd say before launching into her latest rant. "Aboriginal people in Canada pay 5 billion dollars in taxes, but the total amount the government spends on 'Indians' is only 4 billion . . ."

He'd join in, and hours would pass while they plotted to change the world. They'd tell each other funny stories, give each other glimpses of the dreams they kept closest to their hearts, let each other peek at the failures and heartaches they'd endured. After hours, they would hang up, still with words to say.

As months passed, I thought more and more about erotica, and my longing grew. I longed for images and stories of love between our people. Love between people I would recognize. Between Indigenous people like the ones I knew. Not the stereotypes and fantasies of Hollywood or those of sexually bored middle-aged American housewives or of white men looking to affirm their virility and dominance—I wanted something true. If I was going to read fantasies about Indigenous men, I wanted them to be like my fantasies, to stir my desire for flesh-and-blood Indigenous men. I wanted them to be about love, not power.

And now, kneeling before her, with his hand in an alpha female wolf track, was the Anishnaabe man of her prayers. She wanted that same hand to reach into her. To know her ridges and hollows. To recognize her by touch.

She could see his nostrils flare, sniffing the air around her.

She caught her breath. She wanted him, sniffing and pawing at her. Digging up her bones. Hot on her scent.

And slowly I began to write the erotic poems and stories I was unable to find elsewhere. The more fruitless my search for Indigenous erotica, the more I pushed through the layers of fear, doubt and inhibition to write my own erotica. In the midst of this process I fell in love for the first time. Suddenly, the fortress I had built to protect myself came tumbling down, and I felt more intensely connected to the manitouwan, the life force in everything around me. I was euphoric and disoriented. It was like being a stranger in my own homeland. I knew it was where I belonged, and I was joyful, adventurous and uncertain as I set out on a discovery of new places. It was as if I were learning a whole new language—a language that was my Native tongue and yet one that somehow I had never spoken. I felt as if I had some deeper hidden knowledge of it: that it had always been right there, forming my thoughts and feeding my dreams. That it was in my blood and bones, that some memory of it was in my cells, that it was woven into my DNA.

Sky liked her, too—she could tell. He wanted her. He tried not to acknowledge it, but she recognized it in the way his body reacted when she was near him. How his chest puffed out slightly. How his eyebrows waggled up and down when she talked. How the pupils of his eyes dilated. She was aware of how he leaned into her when she spoke. How his body coiled when another man came close to her.

It was obvious if you knew how to look. If you could read the tracks and knew how to decipher the story.

She tried to stop herself, to not be too obvious, but she caught herself flicking her hair. Noticed that they stood just a little closer when they talked to each other. She laughed a little louder, smiled a little bit more. Tilted her head, batted her eyes and touched her hair. A case study in flirting, she thought. A walking, talking cliché. As everyone is when it comes to love.

With him the world seemed wet and vibrant and filled with light, like a moonlit night in spring, when the sap is running and the spring peepers are singing.

And she couldn't help it. She flirted outrageously with him. She was witty. She was fun. She felt the world roll beneath her feet. She could do anything. She would try anything. Charm oozed out of her pores, like honey from a honeycomb. It was beyond her control. She felt madly, crazily, alive. She wanted to stand in the middle of Elgin Street and sing his name. She wanted to climb Blue Mountain and hear his name echo back to her. She wanted to walk the Niagara Escarpment and tell every buzzard and crow to call out his name. She couldn't help it. It was him doing this, not her. It was he who awoke her. It was them, together, who saw sun and stars and moon in each other.

I wrote and wrote trying to find my way to this language. Trying to express this new self, this new world of feeling. Every poem became a love poem. Love infused my thinking, my actions, my world. Every word seemed to pulse. The heartbeat was there in language, in the humming I could hear between trees, in the stones I collected on the shore, in the flickering of stars. I pushed at the barriers inside myself. I had tasted the sweet air of a new freedom and breathed deeply. I wanted to liberate myself. To decolonize myself. Not a victim, not a "survivor," not reactive, not forced into someone else's contorted image of who I was supposed to be, not confined, not colonized. Free.

She tried to imagine what that would be like, to have a lover, a sweetie who was all that and could call out to her in the language. What would he say? She tried to imagine. Men sometimes said the strangest things to her in lovemaking, if they spoke coherently at all.

What would an Anishnaabe man say in Anishnaabemowin? She wasn't sure—but she was damn sure she'd like to find out.

She tried to think of the nicknames he would invent for her. Wondered if he would introduce her as his "buzgim." Or would he use an English word—lover, girlfriend, partner, sweetie . . .? She'd always secretly harboured a desire to be referred to as someone's "sweetie." Even though it was an English word it was such a Nish thing to say. Her toes curled at the thought of it.

What drove me to continue on this quest to bring the erotic back into Indigenous arts? Largely it was that I instinctively knew that the erotic is essential to us as human beings and that it had to take its rightful place in our lives and cultures before we could truly decolonize our hearts and minds.

Looking back I think perhaps I was also unsure how to embrace my sexuality as a Native woman in a healthy, positive way. I had long since rejected the stereotypes and was tired of reacting against them, but I had found few alternatives. My grandparents had a loving marriage and were together for more than fifty years, but I was constantly inundated with negative images, bad news or a pervasive, resounding silence. It had felt safer to be political and Native or creative and Native than to be a Native woman in love and comfortable with her sexual nature. So, at thirty years of age I felt like a newborn, growing and learning and changing. Seeing a world of light, forming new connections in my brain to make sense of it all, learning to speak, taking tentative steps, falling, getting hurt, crying, laughing. Everything seemed new and alive and possible.

He smiled at her. "Would you like to feel the track?"

"Megwetch," she said, moving closer to him.

Why couldn't she have met someone like him years ago? Why now? Why him? He would have been going to his grade 8 grad when she was getting her MA at university. He would have been in diapers

when she was at her grade 8 grad. Now, here she was, longing, dying
to touch him. First with her hands, just her fingertips lightly touching
his face. So softly, her hand would tremble in passing. Then her lips
brushing his cheek before grazing his lips. Her tongue would circle his
mouth before tasting the tip of his tongue. Later her tongue would
travel the entire territory of his body, mapping it with taste and touch.
She would know the smell of him, the texture of the hair on the inside
of his thighs, the taste of him, the size and feel of him in her mouth,
resting on her tongue. She would know the friction of him, feel the
wetness, reach down to the spark igniting.

She would learn to recognize him with just one touch.

When I landed in Penticton to teach creative writing, strung out
on love and lust, thousands of kilometres from my lover, I sought
escape in the arts. I wanted to be surrounded with images, songs,
artwork and literature that could inspire me and help me to maintain those powerful feelings that I had never connected with
before. I wanted to read erotica by and about Indigenous people.
I wanted to see myself and my lover reflected. I wanted to read
erotica, to write erotica, to live it. I wanted it because I wanted to
find a way back to the erotic in myself. To be fully alive. Literature was a compass, pointing me home.

It was true. Sky's youth was a turn-on. She'd be lying if she didn't
admit that. But if it were just that, she wouldn't be taking her time
like this. If it had just been about sex with a hot young body, it
could've been wham-bam, over and done with long ago. But it was
more than that. He was precious and beautiful to her. She loved the
firmness of his body, smooth tautness of his skin, his ease and grace-
fulness. His strength and playfulness. His way of seeing the world. It
made her feel beautiful, too. Rather than feeling old, as some other
younger men made her feel, being near him allowed her to appreciate
both his youthful energy as well as her own hard-won maturity and

calmness. Looking at him, she loved the lines that were starting to etch around her eyes and mouth when she smiled, the stories she was able to tell about her travels, her triumphs and her losses. She loved the feeling of ripening that possessed her body. She could see how it mesmerized him in the same way that his vigour intoxicated her. She felt more vital, and he seemed more serene.

Where was the erotica I so longed for? Where were those images of love and passion between Indigenous people? They were so scarce. In fact, they were so well hidden I finally started to talk to other writers about erotica and whether they knew of any or had written or created any themselves. For me, erotica became a medicine that would help to heal those broken and forgotten parts of who we are. It was an antidote to the Disney Pocahontas, to *Once Were Warriors*, to the residential school stories that haunted us, to the fear Native girls are taught, to the bone-chilling news about missing and murdered Native women, to the shame so many of us had learned growing up Native, growing up Native and female, growing up Native, female and Roman Catholic, to the revelations of sexual abuse by a priest in our communities, to the stereotypes and caricatures of Hollywood and Harlequin, to the government-imposed labels and laws that were designed to bind us. If erotica could help to heal something in me, I knew that many other Indigenous people shared my experiences and would reach for it, too.

She'd had other lovers—Indigenous lovers from various nations, White lovers, Black lovers, Asian lovers, lovers who were wonderful glorious mixes and combinations of all kinds . . . She'd even thought she loved one or two of these men. But not one, not even the Native ones, had ever called her his sweetie. Long ago, she'd believed she'd only ever have Anishnaabe lovers. She didn't want children who were caught between two worlds the way she had been. Called a "non-

Status Indian." Not her kids. No way. She wanted to be able to give them that much at least.

But love is not so rational. It doesn't give a damn about racist legislation, Indian Acts, Band Membership or Treaty Rights. And lust is even less judicious.

She'd mostly found herself alone when her Anishnaabe-only love policy was in place. She soon realized that politics is politics and love is love and you can't force yourself to love someone, or for them to love you, just so that your future children would get Status cards.

"It was a crazy idea caused by the insidious policies of a racist government," she told Mike. But still she always wished love had worked out that way, and deep down she'd longed for a man who could talk to her in the language. Who would call her his sweetie and make scone for her. Who would dry fish and skin deer and make offerings for her health and safety. Who would sing lullabies to their children in Anishnaabemowin. She wanted a man at home on the land. Grounded.

In the midst of my awakening, as I searched for erotic literature, continued writing it and began, slowly, to talk to others about it, I met a young Métis poet named Greg Scofield. I doubt that we talked about erotica in the many hours we spent at that kitchen table, talking. But when his new book of poetry *Love Medicine and One Song* came out the following year, I devoured it. I felt affirmed and elated. I savoured those poems. Remembered what it had been like to be in love, to touch my lover's body, to feel my own unfurl and stretch in the warmth and light of this new sun. Although I was already writing and collecting erotica, those poems touched something inside me.

One touch after months spent carefully not touching. They'd gone to great lengths to ensure they never touched each other. As if both of them knew what it would mean. If one so much as brushed past the other, or if they sat beside one another and their legs touched for even a moment, that small patch of skin would tingle and come alive, and they'd move immediately as if they feared one of them would sponta- neously combust.

"But Officer," she could hear herself saying, "I only just barely touched him for an instant."

Just one touch. That's all it would take.

One touch to begin the story.

One touch to start the migration.

One touch to seed the rain clouds.

One touch to set off lightning storms.

One touch to ignite the frenzy.

Greg's poems reminded me that although love affairs may begin and thrive in beauty and may, sometimes, end in tumult, to express love opens us in a way that can never be completely closed again. I loved to be in love. I loved who I was in love. I loved sex and embraced my sexuality in a way I had not been able to before that time. I began to love myself and the people and world around me with more compassion and passion. Before this I had lived, primarily, in my head. Being in love taught me that I was physical, emotional and spiritual as well as intellec- tual and that all aspects of my being needed to be healthy and in balance. Despite my flaws and imperfections, my scars and weaknesses, I felt beautiful and whole. Despite being Anish- naabe and a woman and knowing all too well how dangerous that could be, I had finally let go of shame and fear in favour of love. *Love Medicine and One Song* inspired me to keep writing erotic poetry and stories that felt true to me and my reality as an Anishnaabe woman.

The first day she met Sky at an airport in Winnipeg, she had noticed how his brown eyes had flecks of gold that turned green when he exerted himself. She imagined herself staring into those eyes as he

spread her legs and slid into her. Imagined how hard it would be
to look away. Ever.

Since Greg and I met we have read together, written together,
performed together, laughed together and become close friends.
Over the years we have talked often about love and erotica. In
2003 we co-wrote and performed a thirty-minute radio piece
about erotica called "Beneath the Buffalo Robe" for CBC Radio
One. As we spoke during that piece Greg reminded me that
erotica is "about creating new medicine." He went on to say,
"it's about creating new stories and new songs based upon those
experiences, healing with those things and allowing ourselves to
become whole and healthy individuals." As writers we are taking
our knowledge and experiences as Indigenous people from rich
and vibrant cultures, as people who have been colonized, stereo-
typed, violated and abused, and through our erotic stories and
poems we are transforming all of that into something affirming,
inspiring and beautiful.

"If you touch the inside of the tracks very gently, you'll learn to recog-
nize the feel of them."
    She watched him speak as if she were the most attentive, serious
student in the group of would-be trackers. All the while thinking how
she loved the colour of his lips, imagined how they would feel on her
neck, breasts, and belly. Imagined them gently touching the deepest,
most secret places inside of her.

Of course, what we consider beautiful and what we consider
erotic is partly personal and partly culturally determined. Our
values and aesthetics are influenced by our families, our communities, our histories and the society around us. Indigenous erotica
is what it is because it reflects the values and aesthetics of those
Indigenous cultures out of which it is created.

His name was Sky. She saw a sunrise in his smile. She saw a starbright night in his eyes. When he spoke, she felt as if his voice resonated inside of her. He spoke to her about how birds, animals and humans had once been able to speak the same language.

She became a hawk spreading her wings over him. Circling.

He had long black hair that he usually kept in a ponytail. She day-dreamed about seeing his hair loose, spread out against the sparkling white of freshly washed linens. Smiling as she rode him. His hips buck-ing and her leaning back and into him, pressing her thighs into his sides. Her smiling back at him and the two of them laughing as he pushed into her. His skin, dark and glistening beneath her golden brown skin. Then she would lie beside him, and they would move together like two wild horses running through fields of fire. She would stamp her feet, and he would rise up, call to her, then nuzzle her neck before they stampeded into the hills and valleys spread out around them.

I have found that Indigenous erotic literature is often an attempt to reach out, to touch and, for a moment, to hold beauty aloft. Much of it is very firmly based in the natural world—it reflects and affirms our connections with other aspects of the natural world, such as animals, birds, plants, the land, the sky, the water, weather, the elements. In doing so it reminds us who we are and that we are intimately connected to all that surrounds us.

"You make me laugh," he told her.

She wanted to throw him on the floor and leave him in a panting, trembling heap. She wanted to Kama Sutra him silly. She wanted him to pin her to the floor, pound her into the earth until she forgot where she began and ended. She wanted to rise up and roll him over, wres-tle him, tickle him, then hold his arms down with her calves, sit on his chest and feel him lapping at the sweetest part of her. She wanted him to take her hand in his and place it firmly on his balls while his tongue flicked into her, like a bear licking honey. Until she had to have him and lowered herself onto his stiff, hard cock, pushing down, down. Until, rising and falling, she became the sun and he became a tree straining upward, reaching for her. Until she vanished into clouds. And he melted into the earth.

I have also noticed that our erotica tends to be much more playful, humorous and joyful than other erotica I have collected and read. In my opinion, humour is one of the most obvious characteristics of Indigenous literary erotica. It abounds in the stories of writers such as Maria Campbell, Richard Van Camp, Basil Johnston, Joseph Bruchac, Kenny Laughton, Briar Grace-Smith and Lesley Belleau; in the poetry of Daniel David Moses, Marilyn Dumont, Wayne Keon, Randy Lundy, Joanne Arnott, Marcie Rendon, Chrystos and Hone Tuwhare, and in the literary expression of many of the other Indigenous writers who have written and published erotica.

It's okay, she told herself. He's an adult. Besides, he's gorgeous, healthy, intelligent, outdoorsy—and he's Anishnaabe. How could she not be drawn to him?

"He even speaks Anishnaabemowin!" she told her cuzzie-bro Mike.

Mike said, "Good. Maybe you'll learn something other than how to call people rude names."

"Or maybe I'll learn a few more to add to my repertoire," she said, winking.

A couple of years ago I created a humorous spoken-word piece with a serious message about beauty and sexuality at its core. In writing and performing it I wanted to celebrate Anishnaabe beauty, our bodies and our ways of relating to each other— which, even in lovemaking, can include teasing and kindness and, at the best of times, an openness and acceptance that is endearing and unbelievably romantic. I was inspired to create it by a brief

conversation I once had with an Anishnaabe man about a particular part of his anatomy. The piece is called "Ode to My Lover's
Flat Indian Ass."

Like many other Anishnaabe people I have often heard
people complain and make jokes about our "flat Indian asses."
As I thought about it I realized how beautiful we are and how
the characteristics that make us Anishnaabek are part of that
beauty—even having a "flat ass." The traits that make us unique,
that are outside of what is considered "conventional beauty" or
the kinds of fake, air-brushed, injected, liposuctioned "beauty"
propagated by pop-culture media, are the very ones that make
us most attractive. Although we joke about them, our "flat asses"
are a part of what makes us distinctly beautiful, and it seemed to
me that they ought to be celebrated and admired. At that moment
I decided to be the first to stand up, say it loud and say it proud:
flat asses are sexy! And so, through a simple spoken word piece,
the humble Anishnaabe poet strives to elevate the lowly "flat ass"
to its rightful place as "a muse, an inspiration, an object of beauty,
a miracle . . ."

Still, her family would tease her when she brought him home. No
doubt.

"So, Win," they'd ask, "how old was he when you were starting
high school?"

They'd ask if he had training wheels on his Harley. If she had to
cut his meat for him or if his mom let him use real knives like a big
boy. They'd call her Demi and him Ashton. They'd yell out things
when they drove by like "where's your Binogeeze-Man?" Or they'd
do things like buy him a Happy Meal and tell her they'd arranged for
Meals on Wheels for her.

Her brother Elwin would put a crib in their room. In the morning
they'd ask if the "baby" kept her up all night, and her brothers would
wink at each other and laugh.

Everyone in the whole community would know five minutes after they arrived and would get in on the teasing.

She wouldn't care. She'd laugh, too. It was funny, after all these years, to find him at all, let alone in such beautiful wrapping. Maybe the timing was a bit off, but hey, the universe works in mysterious ways, and all that mattered to her was that those years of searching, then those years of despairing and giving up the search, had somehow finally led to this. This man. This man kneeling beside her, reaching into the earth.

The spiritual or supernatural world is also often present in the Indigenous erotic literature I know. This is undoubtedly because it reflects our understanding of who we are and places us within a web of connections. For many of us, erotica is not something outside of who we are, or something "other." Rather, it reflects fundamental beliefs about our relationship to all beings and to ourselves.

Sky seemed to like that when he spoke she was riveted; that she watched him watching her; that when he walked into a room she became a cat ready to pounce; that even if she seemed not to be looking she knew when he was near. Lightning bolts flew from her body, and the air between them became an electrical storm front.

Northern lights reflected on the ceiling.

Solar storms turned the sky red.

At dusk, she sprinkled tobacco, thought of it as stardust, and watched the nights lengthen. She thought about old-time stories of humans and Sky People falling in love. Of women watching the night sky, falling in love, and becoming Star People to be with their lovers in the Sky World.

She watched Sky and knew she was made of starlight.

As an Anishnaabekwe descended from a line of orators and storytellers, I have been taught that words are powerful. As I grew,

I came to understand that "love is medicine" and the greatest power in creation. Somehow I also began to understand that writing the erotic could be revolutionary. I came to realize that to bring love and sexuality back to their rightful place in Indigenous societies required a revolution, a re-evolution that would take us back to our beginnings to reclaim our stories and who we are in a powerful and empowering way. I have a dream that there is going to be a generation of our people, hopefully the next generation, who grows up with these positive images, these positive portrayals, these positive people who are comfortable in their own bodies, in their own sexuality and in loving other Indigenous people so that the erotic is simply an accepted, normal part of who they are. That is the legacy I hope we leave, and I want to be in the midst of it, leading when necessary, moving forward with others of similar mind and following in the footsteps of my ancestors and those Indigenous writers who have walked this path ahead of me.

As he kneeled there, showing her how to touch the wolf track, she noticed the skin on the knuckles of his hand, the sparkle of stars in his eyes. She wanted to throw herself on him, rip their gear off and roll with him in the snow and mud, until they had to run, their hearts pounding as they shivered and danced in the cold April air. She wanted to take his hand and run until they couldn't run anymore, then their bodies, spent, gasping for breath, would collapse to the earth, and they would rise later, blinking into the sun like newly formed beings. Ready to greet a new day, together. And every time they made love they would re-enact this scene and know there was no place else to run. Nothing to hide. New beginnings stretched before them, like the sun reaching across the horizon.

She kneeled beside him. Reached out her hand.

"Just one touch," she thought.

"Just one."

INUIT MEN, EROTIC ART

Certain Indecencies...
That Need Not Here Be Mentioned

Norman Vorano

Curator of Contemporary Inuit Art,
Canadian Museum of Civilization

ONTEMPORARY EROTIC INUIT ART may strike some readers as a contradiction in terms. A casual stroll through a gallery, museum or retail outlet will generally reinforce what July Papatsie described as "the common perception that Inuit art is simply arctic animals and scenes from the past."[1] Although critics and collectors have recently lavished praise upon a small number of Inuit artists for their increasingly daring and dynamic exploration of themes, styles, materials and practices, the appearance of erotic Inuit art—especially art made by Inuit *men*—remains conspicuously rare.

This near absence invites a number of questions—some historical, some terminological, some speculative. Is the perception that erotic Inuit art is scarce entirely justified? (For the sake of space, we will have to accept this assumption more or less at face value.) What pressures exert upon men to restrict the production of erotic artworks? Moreover, how do we define the term *erotic*?

Must an erotic image depict explicit sex, or does our concept of the erotic shift over time? Is it possible to extricate Euro–North American notions of eroticism from those that may belong to Inuit? Last, what can we conclude regarding the relations of power, discourse and sexuality in art and culture? These questions are open ended and yet complexly related; undoubtedly it is beyond the scope of this essay to do each of them justice. But taken together, they begin to delineate a particular issue concerning both Inuit art production and the related discourses about eroticism, sexuality, gender and Inuit art.[2] By "discourses," I mean those regulatory systems of representation through which European and North American audiences produced their knowledge of and made meaningful statements about Inuit masculinity and sexuality at particular historical moments. Discourses about Inuit sexuality define the audience's horizon of expectations; by exploring these structures of thought we can better understand the rules of exclusion that narrowed—and eventually expanded—opportunities for Inuit men to express sexual or erotic themes in their art.

A number of mutually reinforcing factors explain why sexuality has been, and continues to be, one of the most tentative and equivocal sites for configuring male Inuit artistic identities since the 1950s. Historically, the systemic *Qallunaat* (white) misapprehension and denigration of Inuit sexuality, followed by the pervasive trafficking in the "happy-go-lucky Eskimo," created a flattened and manifestly *asexual* stereotype about Inuit masculinity in the south. These *Qallunaat* cultural dispositions indirectly shaped the production of Inuit art through their articulation in the marketplace. In a more direct way, the desexualization of Inuit art was influenced, first, by the missionary work in the Arctic and, second, the residential school experience, which, for some Inuit, instilled a sense a shame about Inuit culture in general and sexuality more specifically.

Inuit male artists, more so than women artists, have had to submit their work to a public that for over a half century openly trafficked in neotenous stereotypes of Inuit masculinity. These damaging stereotypes diminished the possibility for audiences to recognize, understand or sympathize with the many emotional valences of male Inuit eroticism. Instead, *Qallunaat* preconceptions of Inuit sexuality served to weaken the affective affinities between audience and artist—bonds that are necessary for viewers to identify with "thicker" human experiences: love, eroticism, desire and sexuality. But the grip of stereotype is not total; some male Inuit artists have worked against the grain of expectations to explore sexual or erotic themes in their artwork, and I shall look at three of them in this essay. This, I hope, will offer episodic glimpses into more contemporary relations of sexuality and discourse in the Inuit art world and the means by which artists challenge these relations.

THE TRAFFIC IN INUIT ART

"Contemporary Inuit arts," as I use the phrase, refers to a diverse category of objects made for sale to a southern market, including carvings, prints, drawings, fabric arts and ceramics. Numerous researchers have chronicled the historical emergence of the Inuit art markets in the modern era,[3-5] which formally started in 1949 and involved multiple sites of production, distribution and consumption. They have mapped the linkages between government officers and private entrepreneurs, "middlemen" such as James Houston, artists from various northern communities, southern wholesale distribution outlets and a disparate system of galleries, critics and buyers. Of all scholars, the anthropologist Nelson Graburn has most closely examined the processes of selection and exclusion that are part and parcel of this system,[6] underscoring how prevailing *Qallunaat* discourses of "authenticity"—and we might also add tacit assumptions about sexuality—have powerfully influenced patterns of production, distribution and consumption.

Scholars including Myers[7] and Phillips and Steiner[8] have developed theories regarding this dialogical approach to the world-art art world, and they have mapped the differential relations of power within the art–culture system. Artist, middleman, gallery owner, anthropologist, art historian, audience and buyer—each of these agents possesses different value systems and draws upon his or her own set of cultural, social and gender-based dispositions to influence how cultural texts are created, distributed and interpreted. As these scholars patently demonstrate, audiences are not passive participants in the art world; their collective imagination defines "fields of possibility," to use the words of Arjun Appadurai,[9] and, in turn, provide pivotal channels through which artists must negotiate their "local" cultural traditions, however those traditions are defined.

Although Inuit and First Nations peoples in Canada share a colonial history, the circumstances involving Inuit artists are in many ways significantly different from those of their First Nations counterparts. Since the 1950s, artmaking has become—and still is today—the single largest source of income for many Inuit families. Artmaking is such an entrenched part of the northern economy that it is sometimes held as a panacea for northern economic development. Inuit artists are subjected to the restrictive rules of the marketplace and the mediating effects of the co-operatives; moreover, few have enjoyed the shelter of artist grants or university teaching posts, where they may be more able to pursue challenging or culturally sensitive themes without the incessant pressure to "turn a sale." For instance, art historians have remarked upon the discrepancy between the highly personal, unpublished drawings made by Inuit women artists and the types of images that are routinely published as prints for wide sale through co-operatives.[10] Unmoored from the print world, the

Cape Dorset artist Napachie Pootoogook, now deceased, began in the 1990s to explore in her drawings a variety of themes seldom seen in Inuit art: eroticism, domestic violence, spousal abuse, gender relations.[11] Yet this apparent thematic openness is not spread equally across the gender divide. Male sculptors working within this market-oriented system, as Graburn aptly surmised, "live in a minefield of rules that they overstep at their peril."[12]

SEX, TRAVEL AND THE NINETEENTH-CENTURY ARCTIC

Representations of Inuit run deep in the *Qallunaat* imagination, as does the root of the issue. Having intermittent contact from the late sixteenth century, *Qallunaat* and Inuit encountered one another with intensified frequency after the Napoleonic wars, when England resumed its quest for the famed Northwest Passage with renewed vigour. William Parry's first "over winter" in 1820 inaugurated more frequent and prolonged contact between Europeans and Inuit, which resulted in a slew of widely distributed and highly influential travel narratives, punctuated by richly detailed verbal descriptions and vivid images of Inuit.[13] Historian Robert David has shown how these and many other nineteenth-century representations of the Arctic in the British imagination, abetted by the explosive growth of mass media and the rise of public exhibitions, were tied to the imperial and economic ambitions of Britain in the Arctic.[14] Sexuality became one of many narrative subtexts in the "civilizing mission" that was the British colonial drama at home and abroad. Unsurprisingly, Inuit courtship and marriage customs caught the attention of these *Qallunaat* interlopers, mainly naval men with Christian backgrounds. Their accounts, voraciously consumed by a curious public, betray their heteronormative assumptions about gender identity, male privilege and monogamy.

Inuit "spousal swapping" elicited nearly unanimous condemnation. William Parry remarked upon this practice during his voyages to the eastern Canadian Arctic in the 1820s. Like many of his contemporaries, Parry struggled to reconcile his ethnographic observations with his Christian moral code. Although he acknowledged the "practicality" of spousal exchange during long seasonal trips, Parry also remarked that he "cannot give a very favourable account of the chastity of women, nor of the delicacy of their husbands."[15] He explained:

> As for the latter, it was not uncommon for them to offer their wives as freely for sale as a knife or a jacket. Some of the young men informed us that, when two of them were absent together on a sealing excursion, they often exchanged wives for the time, as a matter of friendly convenience; and, indeed, without mentioning any other instances of this nature, it may safely be affirmed, that in no country is prostitution carried to greater lengths than among these people. The behaviour of most of the women when their husbands were absent from the huts, plainly evinced their indifference towards them, and their utter disregard of connubial fidelity. The departure of the men was usually the signal for throwing aside restraint, which was invariably resumed on their return."[16]

His reproach was not uncommon. Inuit sexuality, and its supposed "disregard of connubial fidelity," challenged the European concept of the nuclear family—the ideological mechanism for socially reproducing bourgeois concepts of private property, gender inequality and "the nation." Despite the regulatory patterns clearly evident in their writings, Parry and his contemporaries sometimes betray a surprising degree of latitude towards the sexual attitudes encountered in the Arctic. No doubt this sympathy, at least in part, owes to these travellers' "soft primitivism": the romantic and contradictory view that indigenous people lived an unspoiled (if climatically harsh, in the case of Inuit) prelapsarian life, unencumbered by stultify-ing and sometimes "effete" European social codes.

In most cases, whenever Inuit eroticism was described in print or image, it was characterized in prurient and judgmen-tal terms, measured only in relation to a European standard. Such commentary became so commonplace by the early nine-teenth century that explorer John Ross need not bother to pass judgment on his guide's polyandrous wife in his 1835 travel nar-rative; after offering a few titillating details, Ross retreated from his explication and took the moral high ground, safely assured that his readers would pass appropriate judgment themselves. Ross wrote:

> Others must consider for themselves, of the propriety or delicacy of such a connexion as that of two brothers with a single wife, since I do not set up for the moral commentator on a people, respecting whom every one is now nearly as well informed as myself; so much has been written respecting them by us, the recent northern navigators, and by many more, for-eigners as well as English.[17]

Curiously, Ross's comment acknowledges the ubiquity and popular appeal of Inuit representations circulating in Europe while simultaneously underscoring the paradox of Inuit eroticism, which appeared mainly as an absent presence in these nine-teenth-century documents, lurking between the written lines, seldom made explicit. As an example, during the long hours of winter darkness, British naval officers noticed that games, when played by adults, could be a pretense for erotic dalliances. While camped around Igloolik, Parry observed an adult version of the children's game "blind man's bluff" played by a group of Inuit women: having been selected by the group, a woman voluntarily closed her eyes and, amidst the laughter her friends, groped around the *iglu* until she identified a partner. Without spelling out the intimate details, Parry noticed this game invariably gave rise to "very expressive signs which need not here be mentioned," followed by "certain indecencies, with which their husbands are not to be acquainted."[18]

These views became codified during the Victorian era, when an increasingly complacent bourgeois class shored up its moral stability by "medicalizing" notions of proper sexuality and hardening concepts of racial difference. Repressing and recording sexuality became two sides of the same regulatory coin. Foucault's *History of Sexuality* spelled out this paradox in arguing that the political, economic and technical incitement to talk about sex, "not so much in the form of a general theory of sexuality as in the form of analysis, stocktaking, classification, and specification, of quantitative or casual studies,"[19] coincided with the heightening restriction of sex. Missionaries and some anthropologists shared in these shifting attitudes towards sexuality, expressed in their work in the North. Each shaped views about Inuit sexuality in powerful ways, influencing the general public and Inuit alike.

The impact of the missionaries was dramatic. According to the late artist and writer Alootook Ipellie, the arrival of the missionaries "was the beginning of the end of traditional Inuit ideology," when formerly "superstition and taboo ruled every part of Inuit life."[20] Although the first Moravian missions were established in 1771 in Nain, Labrador, most Roman Catholic and Anglican missions arrived over a century later, at the close of the nineteenth century, along with the whalers and the Hudson's Bay Company factors. The transition to Christianity happened abruptly, and sometimes in advance of the missionaries; by the beginning of the twentieth century, with the introduction of alcohol already weakening the stability of families, the work of conversion in the Arctic was mostly complete—but not total.[21]

Missionaries did not take a dispassionate interest in the sexual comings and goings of their new and potential converts in the North; their effect upon sexuality was direct, yet undoubtedly complex. Having prevailed upon Inuit to forsake their traditional beliefs and adopt the laws of God, the priests pushed many of the sexually charged or overly salacious (according to Judeo-Christian standards) folk tales underground. They usurped the authority of the *angakkuit* (shamans)—the "spiritual advisor, healer and mystical leader"[22]—whose traditional duties also included directing the seasonal Tivajuut festival: a communal mid-winter solstice ceremony involving spousal exchange.[23] Although the missionaries did record many shamanistic beliefs and helped Inuit long before the government provided basic social services, they also instilled a negative view towards their "pagan" past.[24] As the Canadian surveyor of the Arctic, Albert P. Low, reported to the federal government in 1906, "The missionaries are exerting their influence to make the Eskimos monogamous." Surprisingly sensitive to the communal benefits of polyandry in the Arctic, Low admonished the missionaries by adding, "This is probably a mistake."[25] In later years, a negative sexual self-image was exacerbated for some Inuit during their residential school experiences, beginning in the 1950s, during which time the missionaries initiated a forced unlearning of Inuit culture. Tragically for some, the residential school experience was accompanied by sexual abuse.

In contrast to the missionaries, early modern anthropologists[26] aimed to move beyond the moralistic and hierarchical evolutionary theories that oriented Victorian anthropology (wedded as it once was to the Christian *scala naturae*). Anthropologists related sexuality to broader theories of social structure and metaphysical and religious cosmology, a method of investigation that was aided by the burgeoning field of sexology and, by the early twentieth century, Freudian psychiatry. Marcel Mauss and Henri

Beuchat's canonical 1906 publication, *Seasonal Variation of the Eskimo: A Study in Social Morphology*, is one of the earliest efforts to understand the function of Inuit spousal exchange in non-evolutionary terms, regarding it as a lever to seasonally regulate social structures between winter communism and summer individualism. But anthropologists and sex have been strange bedfellows, simultaneously proximate and distant, passionate and scientific.[27]

Similarly, sexual relations between *Qallunaat* visitors and Inuit women (and men) were censured in "polite society" in the south, although some Inuit women found that such a relation could be economically advantageous in the North. Napachie Pootoogook completed a small number of drawings in the 1980s in which she recounted the sometimes exploitative side of these encounters.[28] Within these "ethnosexual frontiers," to use a phrase coined by historian Joane Nagel, sexual depictions of racial others and the regulation of endogamy were mechanisms by which European interlopers constructed and maintained ethnic boundaries.[29] For an arctic example, we need only look at the famed ethnologist and navigator Vilhjalmur Ṣtefansson; on his second voyage into the western Arctic from 1908 to 1912, Stefansson took Fannie Pannigabluk, an Alaskan Inuvialuit woman who worked as his trusted seamstress and key ethnological informant, as his arctic wife.[30] Their son, Alex, was born in 1910. Although Stefansson quietly maintained support payments over the decades, he kept knowledge of Alex from the public eye after he returned south, even after he published extraordinarily popular and "scientific" ethnological tracts about the Arctic and the Inuit. His intercultural romance with Pannigabluk—not uncommon for men in the Arctic—was a casualty of bourgeois and colonial sexual attitudes that restricted the mixing of Inuit and *Qallunaat*. Although there were no laws on the books forbidding Inuit and *Qallunaat* to marry in Canada, people who worked in the North were openly forbidden to marry across the cultural division. This informal restriction persisted well into the mid-twentieth century.

SEXUAL ANXIETIES AND THE "HAPPY-GO-LUCKY ESKIMO" IN THE EARLY TWENTIETH CENTURY

From the late nineteenth century until the 1950s, the dominant representation of Inuit in the *Qallunaat* imagination was the "happy-go-lucky Eskimo," ubiquitous in popular films, books, newspapers and advertisements. Childlike, insouciant and yet completely self-reliant, Robert Flaherty popularized (though did not invent) this figure in his 1922 blockbuster film, *Nanook of the North*—"The most cheerful people in all the world," wrote Flaherty in the film's intertitles, "the fearless, lovable, happy-go-lucky Eskimo." Although anthropologists have dissected the accuracy, as well as cultural, political and commercial implications of the "happy-go-lucky" figure,[31-34] there has been only nominal speculation about the sexualized connotations associated with this representation. Related to this, Anthropologist Ann Fienup-Riordan briefly noted that, for representations of Inuit *women* in early Hollywood film, the dominant sexual stereotype consisted of the "sultry maiden lounging in fur inside her igloo," who is "childlike, mysterious, sexy, and natural (without artifice)—simultaneously the innocent caretaker and the exotic primitive."[35] But what are the effects of this representation on *Qallunaat* perceptions of *male* Inuit sexuality? The male "happy-go-lucky" figure, as I will show in further detail below, was related to anxieties about miscegenation, normative assumptions about male sexuality and a simultaneously brackish and anodyne view of Inuit male eroticism.

Few white women travelled into the Arctic before the Second World War. Accordingly, popularized representations of the Arctic in books, films and advertisements clearly illustrated the

North as a male-dominated space, where "arctic explorers not only embodied the epitome of manliness, they turned the poles into theaters of male rivalry," according to Stefansson scholar Gísli Pálsson.[36] The Inuit men and women who were essential for white travel and survival in the North—shipmates, hunters, seamstresses and guides—were virtually written out of the dominant narratives of discovery, pushed to the extreme peripheries of most ethnographic texts or infantilized in advertising stereotype. The "happy-go-lucky Eskimo" must be seen in relation to the *Qallunaat* culture of arctic travel, in which the boundaries between white explorers, and between white explorers and their Inuit male counterparts, were continually policed and reproduced through desexualized representations of the Inuit male. Very often, these representations of Inuit males were depicted in the popular imaginary as "cute"; rarely were they seen as sexually assertive, least of all in the presence of non-Inuit travellers.

But "cuteness," according to Gary Genosko's cultural analysis, is not inert.[37] Genosko draws upon the theoretical work of Stephen J. Gould and the ethnologist Konrad Lorenz to argue that cuteness solicits from its audience "a kindly aggressivity, a giddy proprietary right to possess." Put simply, "cuteness sells," says Genosko.[38] Beyond its capacity to structure forms of mass consumption, these "regimes of cuteness" as Genosko calls these patterns of representation, are "a means by which maturation is stalled or suspended" in the depicted subject. By analogy, the infantilized "happy-go-lucky Eskimo," predicated upon a similar lack of sexual development, becomes a foil against which the *Qallunaat* traveller can safely identify himself as heroic, virile and innately more powerful than his Inuit counterpart. "You'll love these kids," wrote the print advertisement for *Nanook of the North*, "Cute and happy-hearted, they go 'belly-wopping' down an iceberg. They play with the puppies. They eat raw meat . . . you'll laugh! You'll thrill!"[39] The routine denial of coevalness between *Qallunaat* and Inuit in matters of sexual maturation is tantamount to a denial of Inuit male agency, including political agency, in the decades when the "empty" Arctic was thought to lie waiting to be conquered by European men.

Inuit sexuality has occupied a contradictory and unstable place in the *Qallunaat* imagination: offensive but titillating, censured but studied, ubiquitous but rendered invisible. Given these circumstances, and the obligation by artists to validate their cultural identities within the restrictive parameters of the marketplace, it is not surprising that male sexual desire did not become a reflective focal point for many contemporary Inuit artists.

EROTICISM IN TWENTIETH-CENTURY INUIT ART

There have been brief outpourings of "erotic" Inuit art in the North since the 1960s. In Puvirnituq, the Oblate missionary who helped found the Povungnituk Sculptors' Society (later the La Fédération des Coopératives du Nouveau Québec, or FCNQ), Father André Steinmann, encouraged artists to portray traditional Inuit mythologies, even when those stories included sex, nudity and scatological humour. Artists such as Charlie Arnaituq Sivuaraapik and Davidialuk Alaasuaq Amittuq produced an array of carvings illustrating these stories, which were previously frowned upon by the more prudish Anglican missionaries within the community. Graburn notes that Steinmann's approach, his brand of "earthy, French, sensual romanticism,"[40] stood in stark contrast to the repressive (and rival) Anglican missionaries and contributed to the valorization of these types of expressions within the community. But the artworks had little presence in the wider marketplace and were mainly available to curious visitors to Steinmann's post.

The artmaking contest that Graburn staged in Puvirnituq in fall 1967 more clearly illustrates how the nexus of middlemen, artists and consumers' desires plays into the creation and marketing of erotic Inuit art. Shortly after arriving in the community, Graburn noticed that many artists felt an underlying malaise as they repetitiously churned out carvings of hunting scenes and arctic animals for sale to the co-operative, which was the main wholesale buyer in the community. In an effort to "separate [the artist's] own ideas and aesthetics from that they perceived the buyers to have,"[41] Graburn assembled a group of *Qallunaat* judges in the community and offered prizes to the most different—*adjigiingituk*—or imaginative—*takushurnaituk*—carving submitted to the co-operative. He distributed a flyer, written in Inuktitut, around the community, and soon over sixty carvings poured in for the contest. Unencumbered by the demands to sell their carvings, the artists created works through which three themes clearly emerged—"mixtures of human and animal forms; sex; and religion"[42]—although drawing a rigid line between them is nearly impossible. Graburn noted that sexual artworks were often mixed with traditional mythologies and humour, a pattern that is consonant with Lee-Ann Martin's observation about contemporary First Nations erotic art elsewhere.[43]

Eli Sallualuk Kenuajuak, a formally inventive and technically gifted artist, took the first prize. Graburn recalled that his first entry was a stone carving of an Inuit couple having sexual intercourse: "the humor was apparent in the folded skin and wrinkled faces of the obviously old couple."[44] Kenuajuak returned several days later to add another entry to the contest: a stone carving of a couple lying in bed, winking. After that, he added a nude Cyclops sporting an enormous penis, with a wrinkled, elderly woman seated astride it (now in the Winnipeg Art Gallery). Other artists in the community were inspired by Kenuajuak's work and the interest that grew out of the contest. Soon, more artists began to explore the rarely depicted triad of sex, myth and humour.

One such artist was Peter Iqalluq Angutigirk, who entered *Crouching Male Spirit* in the contest (see fig. 1, overleaf). It is a

Figure 1. Peter Iqalluq Angutigirk, CROUCHING MALE SPIRIT 1967, Puvirnituq, soapstone, Canadian Museum of Civilization IV-B-1396, 75-4512.

compact, armless squatting figure with two dog faces emerging from its back. The creature's penis dangles prominently between its legs. The carving possibly illustrates one facet of the well-known myth of Sedna (or Nuliajuk), a complex, varied story that recounts the life of the underwater goddess and progenitor of marine mammals. As a young, beautiful woman, Sedna was reluctant to marry—although she was courted by many suitors. Her father grew steadily frustrated with his daughter's refusal, until the day arrived when a well-dressed stranger visited Sedna and captured her heart. They soon married. Shortly thereafter, the new husband revealed himself to be her father's dog, which had transformed itself into a human. It may be this moment we see captured in Peter Iqalluq Angutigirk's carving. To continue this narrative, Sedna's father banished her to the bottom of the sea because of her transgression. As many hunters have said, it is sometimes necessary to placate Sedna by tenderly, erotically combing her hair in order to coax the marine mammals out, thus ensuring a successful hunt. The exposed genitals in Angutigirk's carving were a frank and humorous reminder that sexuality courses through many traditional Inuit stories, although missionaries sternly discouraged it. Yet, unmoored from the immediate demands of the marketplace, or at least from the artist's perception of *Qallunaat* expectations, artists have more openly investigated this nexus of sexuality, humour and mythology. These works produced by Puvirnituq artists raise questions about the imposition of sexual taboos, be it directly through the missionaries or as negotiated through the marketplace.

It was immediately evident to the Puvirnituq co-operative managers that the new carvings had a historical significance, although their status as "authentic" Inuit art was hotly debated by art critics at the time. George Swinton, an eminent historian of Inuit art, recalled that Inuit art aficionados dubbed many of the carvings stemming from Graburn's contest "weirdo art" and that the works were excluded from the blockbuster, government-sponsored, world-touring exhibition titled Masterworks of the Canadian Arctic: "the first, and perhaps definitive, exhibition of what today is recognized to be 'the best' of three-dimensional art produced in the Canadian Arctic during the past twenty-eight hundred years," wrote Swinton in 1972.[45] Ironically, some of these sexually explicit carvings were quickly snapped up by *Qallunaat* who were working in Puvirnituq, even before judging could be completed.

In the wider art world the Puvirnituq erotic carvings from the late 1960s would have resonated with Canada's cultural *cognoscenti*, still reeling from the morality squad's raid on Dorothy Cameron's downtown Toronto contemporary art gallery in 1965. Cameron's obscenity charge, which she received after an exhibit of seven nude erotic paintings by the artist Robert Markle, became a rallying point around which artists and activists coalesced in Canada, many of whom drew their intellectual energy from a fermenting debate about revolutionary sexual politics. Cameron lost her appeal in the Ontario Supreme Court and was eventually denied an appeal at the Supreme Court of Canada. Before the dust had settled on the Cameron case, in 1967, the Vancouver gallery owner Douglas Christmas was also slapped with an obscenity charge for a David Mayrs's painting *La Dildo*, which further galvanized the fight between champions of expression and censorship. The interest in erotic Inuit art confirmed a nostalgic longing for pre-European sexual and political possibilities. It is ironic, and perhaps an expression of imperialist nostalgia, that these possibilities were embraced through acts of consumption, and long after the work of conversion had been safely accomplished in the North. Yet viewers were also attracted to the sheer novelty of these erotic carvings, because they offered something fresh in the then twenty-year-old marketplace of Inuit art.

The social biography of Peter Iqalluq Angutigirk's carving reveals much about the workings of institutional power, discourse and eroticism in the art world at the time. Neither was *Crouching Male Spirit* sold to a private individual working in the community, nor did it follow the "normal" marketing route for Inuit art. The Puvirnituq Co-operative purchased Angutigirk's carving and then shipped it south to the FCNQ offices in Lévis, the wholesale distribution outlet for Inuit art produced in Nunavik. Under normal circumstances, the FCNQ would sell carvings to private galleries or dealers. Artworks would then fan out from major galleries to individual homes, offices and museums around the globe. However, as the FCNQ directors saw the novel works arriving from Puvirnituq, they set aside roughly twenty-five carvings, most of which were the direct outcome of Graburn's contest (including Angutigirk's *Crouching Male Spirit*). These carvings were earmarked for the National Museum of Man (now the Canadian Museum of Civilization), which had the first opportunity to acquire this unique, historic collection. First exhibited at the National Museum of Man, Angutigirk's *Crouching Male Spirit* was by 1972 being loaned abroad for special exhibits, a move that signalled the new, fresh direction of contemporary Inuit art in the 1970s. Although it was not exhibited in the previously mentioned Masterworks exhibit, art historian George Swinton included it (along with other works stemming from Graburn's experiment) in an exhibition titled Eskimo Fantastic Art, held at the University of Manitoba, which then travelled to the University of Alberta and the Burnaby Art Gallery. Other exhibitions followed. Through the aegis of artists such as Angutigirk and Kenuajuak and the "cultural brokerage" of Graburn, Swinton and their contemporaries, the Inuit art world was starting to thaw.

The influence of this contest spread beyond Puvirnituq. Male artists in many different communities began to explore, in more frank terms than before, erotic and sexual themes. Thomassie Kudluk, an artist from Kangirsuk (Payne Bay), started to produce humorously sexual carvings in the mid 1970s, depicting men and women copulating, exposing body parts and partaking in other erotic activities. Upon his rough-hewn but highly expressive forms, Kudluk would write short titles or captions for his carvings. For example, upon a small carving of a woman (with buttocks exposed) stirring a pot, Kudluk wrote, "If she lets her

Figure 2. Thomassie Kudluk, MAN LOOKING THROUGH TELESCOPE
1976, Kangirsuk, stone, Canadian Museum of Civilization IV-B-1638,
photographer R. Garner, S94-13585.

bare ass show, she's a beautiful woman." Often explicit, his verbal descriptions sometimes evoke ribald double entendres. Upon
a carving of man looking through a telescope, Kudluk explained,
"A man looking through a telescope for a wife, but he is getting
cold" (see fig. 2). Is the man getting "frigid" because of the tem-
perature or because he cannot see a woman?[46] Other carvings
include "Man trying to mount a woman; the woman says she
does not want a skinny man," or simply, "He is trying to make

love to a lady." His cheeky depictions of sexuality were introduced to the public at Toronto's Innuit Gallery of Eskimo Art in 1976, which billed the show as The Eccentric Art of Payne Bay.[47] As a marker of Kudluk's own anomalous position in the Inuit art world, and to further suggest how Inuit sexuality was considered "strange"—even in the "liberated" 1970s—Kudluk's follow-up exhibition in 1978 at the Innuit Gallery in Toronto was called Arctic Oddities, and his 1981 solo exhibit was similarly billed as The Eccentric Art of Thomassie Kudluk.[48] According to the standards of the day, explorations of male sexuality in Inuit carving was labelled "eccentric"; sexual works were, and still are, "oddities." Nevertheless, through exhibitions such as these, audiences have grown more sophisticated in their understanding of Inuit art's cultural complexity and since the 1980s have become more receptive to Inuit erotic art. Artists cleaved open new possibilities for cultural expression. However, like the example from Puvirnituq above, the triad of sexuality, myth and humour was generally facilitated by a sympathetic co-op buyer or supportive patrons, looking to move past the reductive, prescriptive stereotypes that influenced the production of Inuit art from the 1950s.

The increasing sophistication of Inuit art audiences is evident in the growth of numerous short-lived Inuit art fanzines and appreciation societies that sprouted across North America in the early 1980s (the contemporary journal *Inuit Art Quarterly* had its roots in this appreciative culture). The study of Inuit art grew more professionalized as universities began to teach Inuit art history and, in 1982, a Curator of Inuit Art joined the National Gallery of Canada, lending the genre the ultimate stamp of approval in the minds of "cultured" Canadians. The discursive separation of Inuit art and Canadian art was appearing to narrow just as its literal separation did so within the National Gallery. Within this changing receptive milieu, male artists in and around Cape Dorset produced a flurry of erotic artworks.

Unlike many of their predecessors, these Cape Dorset artists began to grow beyond the safety of irony and laughter, which has so often accompanied erotic Inuit art created by men. Tutuyea Ikkidluak was a gifted artist whose life was cut short in 1989. The output of this young man reflects a dynamic personality, an artist who broached both commonplace and rare subjects with confidence and grace. In *Bird and Man* from 1985, Ikkidluak reinterprets the ancient Greek myth (and traditional European artistic idiom) "Leda and the Swan" (see fig. 3). Ikkidluak's highly polished, lyrical sculpture intimates the erotic intensity between woman and animal. This intimacy is central to the Sedna myth, or its variant, the story of Nuliajuk. Nuliajuk is depicted as a chaste maiden who is lured into marriage by a deceptive spirit-bird, whose two offspring migrated south to become the parents of all *Qallunaat* and *Itqiliq* (Cree). Like Sedna, Nuliajuk is the progenitor of all sea mammals, which grew from her dismembered finger joints that fell into the sea. With her body straining forward in a kneeling position, Ikkidluak's sculpture shows the woman's long hair cascading down her shoulders, discreetly covering her exposed breasts. Although he strikes a less humorous tone than previous male artists, Ikkidluak nonetheless expresses the privileged position of male spectatorship in his erotic sculpture. If Ikkidluak is offering a broadly humanistic analogy between Greek and Inuit mythologies (both of which include numerous examples of human–animal copulation), he is exploring the enduring erotic myths that occupy the depths of human imagination and similarly animate many traditional Inuit myths. Artists such as Ikkidluak have brought an increasingly wide range of aesthetic approaches to exploring sexual and erotic themes by male Inuit artists.

CONCLUDING REMARKS

The study of First Nations arts and eroticism is still in its early stages, although the scholarship of Martin and Wood[49] has made

Figure 3. Tutuyea Ikkidluak, WOMAN AND BIRD (LEDA AND THE SWAN)
1985, Cape Dorset, greenstone, Canadian Museum of Civilization
IV-C-6006, D2007-12295.

an important step towards broadening our understanding. They,
and other scholars, have clearly demonstrated that Aboriginal
artists are rejecting the colonial structures of representation that
have kept their erotic art hidden. My own essay is very much a
preliminary discussion; it is nevertheless intended to ground this
ongoing discussion about Aboriginal art, eroticism and desire

upon both discursive and material considerations—the marketplace, audience expectations, sympathetic intermediaries, and so forth. This line of inquiry is important to move beyond idealist notions of "art as cultural reflection," and, mindful of the narrowing assumptions about "discourse," understand how popular discourses about Inuit culture mesh with cultural institutions to provide frames of reference that simultaneously enable and limit what we can say about sexuality.

As Inuit artists, male and female, continue in ever increasing numbers to engage in art that reaffirms their many desires, they simultaneously declare their freedom to explore and express sexuality. For Inuit men, erotic art is still a barrier few have crossed. Although it is inherently difficult for artists to articulate emotions about sexuality under the best of circumstances, it is even more difficult, from the artist's perspective, when artmaking is a main source of personal and communal income. Under this pressure, Inuit male artists have had to submit their work to a critical public that, in historical terms, systematically denigrated their sexual expression. Seen in this light, contemporary erotic Inuit art is not only about personal exploration, but broader political liberation.

NOTES

1 July Papatsie. "Transitions." In *Transitions: Contemporary Canadian Indian and Inuit Art*. Ottawa: Department of Indian and Northern Affairs Canada, 1997: 4.

2 Very briefly, this draws from a larger body of critical theory, notably the work of Judith Butler (*Bodies That Matter*. New York: Routledge, 1993), Eve Kosofsky Sedgwick (*Epistemology of the Closet*. Berkeley: University of California Press, 1990) and Trinh T. Minh-Ha (*Woman, Native, Other: Writing Postcoloniality and Feminism*. Bloomington: Indiana University Press, 1989). These scholars have used Foucault's constructivist approach towards sexuality (*History of Sexuality, vol. 1: An Introduction*. Robert Hurley, trans. New York: Vintage Press, 1977), which viewed the concept of discourse as central to the processes linking sexuality, ideology and social power.

3 Virginia Watt. "In Retrospect." *Inuit Art Quarterly*, Vol. 5, No. 1, Winter 1990: 39–40; "In Retrospect." *Inuit Art Quarterly*, Vol. 4, No. 2, Spring 1989: 42, 44;

"In Retrospect." *Inuit Art Quarterly*, Vol. 4, No. 1, Winter 1989: 37, 38; "In Retrospect." *Inuit Art Quarterly*, Vol. 3, No. 4, Fall 1988: 36, 39; "In Retrospect." *Inuit Art Quarterly*, Vol. 3, No. 3, Summer 1988: 23, 24; "In Retrospect." *Inuit Art Quarterly*, Vol. 3, No. 2, Spring 1988: 27–29, and "In Retrospect." *Inuit Art Quarterly*, Vol. 2, No. 4, Fall 1988: 18–20.

4 Christopher Paci. "Commercialization of Inuit Art: 1954–1964." *Études Inuit Studies*, Vol. 20, No. 1, 1996: 45–62.

5 Helga Goetz. "Inuit Art: A History of Government Involvement." *In the Shadow of the Sun, Perspectives on Contemporary Native Art*. Ottawa: Canadian Museum of Civilization, Canadian Ethnology Services Mercury Series Paper 124: 357–381.

6 Nelson H.H. Graburn. "Authentic Inuit Art: Creation and Exclusion in the Canadian North." *Journal of Material Culture*, Vol. 9, No. 2, 2004: 141–159; "Canadian Inuit Art and Coops: Father Steinmann of Povungnituk." *Museum Anthropology*, Vol. 24, No. 1, 2000: 14–25, and "Ethnic and Tourist Arts Revisited." In *Unpacking Culture: Art and Commodity in Colonial and Postcolonial Worlds*. Ruth B. Phillips and Christopher B. Steiner, eds. Berkeley: University of California Press, 1999: 335–353.

7 Fred R. Myers. "Introduction: The Empire of Things." *The Empire of Things: Regimes of Value and Material Culture*. Santa Fe: School of American Research Press, 2001: 3–61.

8 Ruth B. Phillips and Christopher B. Steiner. "Art, Authenticity, and the Baggage of Cultural Encounter." In *Unpacking Culture: Art and Commodity in Colonial and Postcolonial Worlds*. Berkeley: University of California Press, 1999: 3–19.

9 Arjun Appadurai. *Modernity at Large: Cultural Dimensions of Globalization*. Oxford: Oxford University Press, 1997: 31.

10 Janet Berlo. "Autobiographical Impulses and Female Identity in the Drawings of Napachie Pootoogook." *Inuit Art Quarterly*, Vol. 8, No. 4, Winter 1993: 4–12.

11 Leslie Boyd Ryan and Darlene Coward Wight. *Napachie Pootoogook*. Winnipeg: The Winnipeg Art Gallery, 2004.

12 Graburn, 1999, p. 347.

13 William Parry. *Three Voyages for the Discovery of a Northwest Passage from the Atlantic to the Pacific and Narrative of an Attempt to Reach the North Pole*. New York: Harper, 1844.

14 Robert G. David. *The Arctic in the British Imagination 1818–1914*. Manchester: Manchester University Press, 2000.

15 Parry, p. 216.

16 *Ibid.*, p. 216–217.

17 John Ross. *A Narrative of a Second Voyage In Search of a Northwest Passage ...* Philadelphia: E.L. Carey & A. Hart, 1835: 210.

18 Parry, p. 232.

19 Foucault, p. 24.

20 Alootook Ipellie. "The Colonization of the Arctic." In *Indigena: Contemporary Native Perspectives*. Gerald McMaster and Lee-Ann Martin, eds. Vancouver and Hull: Douglas & McIntyre and the Canadian Museum of Civilization, 1992: 44.

21 Frédéric Laugrand and Jarich Oosten. "Introduction—The Transition to Christianity." In *Inuit Perspective on the 20th Century: The Transition to Christianity*. Victor Tungilik and Rachel Uyarasuk, eds. Iqaluit, NU: Nunavut Arctic College, 1999: 1–17.

22 Ipellie, p. 44.

23 Bernard Saladin d'Anglure. "The Shaman's Share, or Inuit Sexual Communism in the Canadian Central Arctic." *Anthropologica* 35, 1993: 64.

24 Victor Tungilik and Rachel Uyarasuk's rich study, *Inuit Perspectives on the 20th Century, Volume 1: The Transition to Christianity* (Edited by Jarich Oosten and Frédéric Laugrand. Iqaluit, NU: Nunavut Arctic College, 1999), points out that only very recently are people becoming more comfortable to talk about shamanism.

25 Albert P. Low. *The Cruise of the Neptune*. Ottawa: Government Printing Bureau, 1906: 164.

26 Franz Boas, Vilhjalmur Stefansson and Diamond Jenness, among others.

27 The most famous, indeed infamous, example of the confluence between modern anthropology and sexology was Bronislaw Malinowski's 1929 examination of sexuality on the Trobriand Islands, *The Sexual Lives of Savages*. As we know from Malinowski's posthumously published diaries, the phrase "participant observation," which he coined during his South Pacific fieldwork, now evokes an unanticipated double entendre.

28 Jean Blodgett. *Three Women, Three Generations: Drawings by Pitseolak Ashoona, Napatchie Pootoogook and Shuvinai Ashoona*. Kleinburg: McMichael Canadian Art Collection, 1999: 60.

29 Joane Nagel. *Race, Ethnicity and Sexuality: Intimate Intersections, Forbidden Frontiers*. New York: Oxford University Press, 2003.

30 Gísli Pálsson. *Writing on Ice: The Ethnographic Notebooks of Vilhjalmur Stefansson*. Hanover and London: University Press of New England, 2001.

31 Jay Ruby. *A Crack in the Mirror: Reflexive Perspectives in Anthropology*. Philadelphia: University of Pennsylvania Press, 1982.

32 Ann Fienup-Riordan. *Freeze Frame: Alaska Eskimos in the Movies*. Seattle and London: University of Washington Press, 1995.

33 Jay Ruby. "'The Aggie Will Come First': The Demystification of Robert Flaherty." In *Robert Flaherty, Photographer/Filmmaker*. Jo-Anne Birnie Danzker, ed. Vancouver, BC: Vancouver Art Gallery, 1979: 66–73.

34 Alan Marcus. "Images of the Inuit," "Film Imagery of the Happy-Go-Lucky
    Eskimo" and "Nanook Reborn as Joseph Idlout." In *Relocating Eden: The Image
    and Politics of Inuit Exile in the Canadian Arctic*. Hanover, NH: University of
    New England Press, 1995.

35 Fienup-Riordan, p. 62.

36 Pálsson, p. 56.

37 Gary Genosko. "Nature and Cultures of Cuteness." In *Invisible Culture: an
    Electronic Journal for Visual Culture*. Lisa Uddin and Peter Hobbs, eds. Issue 9,
    2005, University of Rochester, New York. Accessed August 10, 2006. http://
    www.rochester.edu/in_visible_culture/Issue_9/genosko.html.

38 In 2004, Madeleine Redfern curated an exhibition held at the Nunatta
    Sunakkutaangit Museum in Iqaluit titled Eskimos in Advertising. The "happy-
    go-lucky Eskimo" was an ideal spokesman for numerous marketing campaigns,
    including Eskimo Pie, Cliquot Club Soda and Up North brand apples, among
    many other products. (See James Sinclair's review in *Inuit Art Quarterly*, Vol. 19,
    No. 2, Summer 2004: 20–22.)

39 Fienup-Riordan, p. 49.

40 Graburn, 2000, p. 23.

41 Nelson Graburn. "Eskimo Carvings and Coops: the Anthropologist as Innovator."
    (unpublished essay). 1970: 9.

42 Diana Trafford. "Takushurnaituk." *North*. Vol. XV, No. 2, March–April 1968:
    521–522.

43 Lee-Ann Martin. "Reclaiming Desire," In *Exposed: Aesthetics of Aboriginal Erotic
    Art*. Regina: MacKenzie Art Gallery, 1999: 44.

44 Graburn, 1970, p. 11.

45 George Swinton. *Eskimo Fantastic Art*. Winnipeg: Winnipeg Art Gallery, 1972: 6.

46 Dorothy Speak. "Catalogue entry for 'Mann mit Teleskop,' by Thomassie
    Kudluk," in *Im Schatten der Sonne: Zeitgenössische Kunst der Indianer und Eskimos
    in Kanada*. Gerhard Hoffmann, ed. Ottawa: Canadian Museum of Civilization,
    1988: 469.

47 The Innuit Gallery of Eskimo Art. *The Eccentric Art of Payne Bay*. Toronto:
    The Innuit Gallery of Eskimo Art, 1976.

48 The Innuit Gallery of Eskimo Art. *The Eccentric Art of Thomassie Kudluk from
    Payne Bay*. Toronto: The Innuit Gallery of Eskimo Art, 1981.

49 Lee-Ann Martin and Morgan Wood (curators). *Exposed: Aesthetics of Aboriginal
    Erotic Art*. Regina: MacKenzie Art Gallery, 1999.

DANCES FOR DOLLARS

Marissa Crazytrain

Small-town Cree girl moves to Toronto to study.
Small-town Cree girl can't survive on student allowance from her band.
Small-town Cree girl needs to supplement income.
The cost of living in the city is higher than she anticipated . . .

A DIMLY LIT HOTEL lounge seems an appropriate place to write about dancing. The Saskatoon Delta Bessborough lounge has that strip club kinda feel, luxurious with low-key elements. Dark overstuffed sofas and ottomans. Shiny slate coffee tables. Even the men sitting here, simply talking to one another, remind me of the clientele of the strip club I use to work at. This place could easily be a strip club. Just erect a few walls . . . add a small stage with a brass pole . . . a DJ who spins stripper music . . . a handful of beautiful girls . . .

Writing about my time as a stripper is so hard. I have to really look inside myself and dig up all that is buried. And I still don't know how I feel about stripping. I made a lotta cash, and it was exciting, but I don't even know if I liked it. It was only a few years back, but it seems like a lifetime ago. I was living a very high-paced lifestyle in Toronto, but now I've come back home to Nowheresville, Saskatchewan, until I figure out what to do next.

My foray into stripping is a delicate subject, not one I can speak about openly, especially around these parts. Nobody around here understands. Other women are not ready to accept it, especially women like my mother, a conservative and lifelong Roman Catholic, who argues that stripping—a word she can barely bring herself to say—is immoral and robs one of one's spirit. My other critics, non-Aboriginal and especially Aboriginal, are on the same page with this one: stripping is wrong, and if you've ever stripped, you're a bad person with no scruples who should be scorned. Period.

That criticism may seem valid, but I disagree with it.

Now, I know that some of you holding this piece of literature in your hand are judgmental types. A lot of people have a problem with nakedness. Some have a big problem with females taking off their clothes for money. That's fine, but if you intend to read any further, you are going to have to open your mind at least 1 per cent. Think of it this way: if you've ever wanted to enter a strip club and not be seen going in, now is your chance. Consider this chapter a brief look at the social experiment I conducted over the course of a year and a half as a stripper.

I won't lie—the first time I danced on stage I was scared. But I also knew that I could do it. The male species is a visual one, and it doesn't take much to arouse a hot-blooded man. That is why the stripping industry will never die. I know, it's unfair on many levels. It's unfair for women—unfair for the ones who aren't brave or beautiful enough to dance, and unfair for the those who are but then get persecuted for the choices they make. What woman wouldn't want to be worshipped for her beauty with money? Celebrities are paid for their beauty all the time.

We put people on billboards and movie theatre screens. "Sex sells," as the old saying goes.

Not a lot of people would pay money to make money; that's why we work in the first place, right? To dance in Toronto you have to acquire a license from the city, which will set you back a few hundred dollars. The municipal government knows the girls will make that back right away. Which I definitely did the first night I danced. I took home five hundred dollars, tax free.

Dancers have to be businesswomen. Private dances cost twenty bucks a song, and the money the girls make on those dances belongs to them. No DJ fee, no management fee—just a twenty-dollar dancing fee you pay when you sign in at the beginning of the night. You can make that back if you do a stage dance: a set of three songs, each three minutes long.

The stage dance is what people usually picture when they think of stripping. They believe that stage dances are lucrative. In truth, unless you've been in the game for long enough that patrons actually put down red and green bills while you do your set on stage, stage dances are more of a marketing strategy. Only a few girls clean up (mind the pun) when they dance on stage. The longer you dance, the better your stage dances get. If a dancer actually likes what she does, it shows on stage and that's how she makes money. You've got to be a good actor and understand what it is to have stage presence. A certain amount of the job requires that you be creative, because, let's face it, stripping is highly competitive—cut-throat, even. One of the most successful stage dances happens when two girls dance together. It's a good way to get the attention of every patron in the club.

But the real money is in private dances, the ones in the little booths. Picking who you will and who you won't dance for is tricky, because you never know what you're going to get once you close that velvet curtain. It's like voting—you have to pick the cleanest of the dirtiest, so to speak.

Yes, dancing is a very high-risk occupation—that's why, when you work at a strip club, you leave yourself behind and assume another identity. You have a stage name and a buffer name. My stage name was Marissa, and if a patron got persistent, I'd give him my buffer name, my pretend real name, "Geraldine." I have a versatile enough look to create a nationality for my dancer persona—half Malaysian and half Italian. It's all part of the job. I never offered any information about my background, unless the patron got it right through some miraculous guess.

I've had a few crazy experiences. Celebrities? The closest one I've come to dancing for is the Canadian version of Simon Cowell on *Canadian Idol*. I told him I was also a singer, and he encouraged me to audition. Lol . . . He tipped generously. The most fucked up thing happened in the middle of a private dance, when this guy pulled out his—you know. I was peeling my thong down to my ankles with my knees locked. I looked back at him through my spread legs, as I always did with every patron, but this guy was pulling his goalie. Hard.

Then he says, "Come on baby, I'll pay you more if you sit down on it!"

I was totally taken by surprise, but I still called a bouncer, and the guy was escorted out of the club.

Many of the men I danced for were nameless, faceless vessels. But there was this one that I'll never forget. It was a busy Friday night in the VIP lounge. I can't recall if I approached him or if he approached me, but we found ourselves in a private dancing booth talking about the NFL Super Bowl, which was approaching in the next few weeks. He told me I could dance, but mostly he just wanted to talk. He told me his name but I forgot it the second he said it. He reminded me of a hit man in a gangster film. He stood at least six foot three, a wall of strength, with a manicured goatee and a bald head. Not to mention his get-up: dressed in black, head to toe. There was something about him;

even though we were where we were, I felt an inkling of safety mixed with uncertainty. Then, after about five songs had passed, he propositioned me.

The Man in Black would pay me five hundred dollars if I joined him for one drink outside the club. That definitely got my attention. My better judgement was saying no, but my curiosity was leaning towards yes. I asked him where, he said he knew a lounge on Queen Street West. One drink, that's all he asked. I knew my place was only a short cab ride away from that street.

I agreed. I got changed and met him outside the club, waiting in a taxi. He noticed how different I looked: hair in a ponytail, wearing normal clothes, sneakers. "You look like a girl." On our way, I felt a little more cautious then I had in the club, a little less confident. When we arrived at Habitat, I wondered how odd we must look together.

There was only a few people around, other than that we were alone. He chose a table and I excused myself to go to the ladies room. Once there I wondered if I should just leave, sneak out the back? I could catch a taxi on the next block! The danger was more apparent in a quiet, virtually empty lounge. One drink, fifteen minutes, he'll pay me and then I'm gone. What kind of person does this? What does he want from me?

I joined the mysterious stranger in black back at the table. I ordered a short rye and coke and he did the same. Sitting there I remained tentative and listened to his conversation. I don't recall exactly what we talked about, but I never told him anything about my real life. I didn't question him about what he did or where he came from, I just wondered what his motive was. He watched me as I finished my drink and he finished his.

Outside the lounge the street was empty and snowy. As I hailed a taxi he produced his wallet and kept his end of the deal. He gave me five crisp hundred-dollar bills and kissed me on the forehead. When the taxi pulled away from the curb I turned around to wave goodbye, but by then the Man in Black had already vanished.

Most of what you know about strippers probably comes from TV, movies and magazines. Unless you live in one of the country's few major centres where most strip clubs are, and you're gutsy enough to walk into one, your chances of seeing a live stripper are slim to none. The Internet doesn't count: it's not *real*. One of the reasons stripping is so alluring is that the girl is real and right in front of you, not flickering on some fifteen-inch monitor.

Why would I ever decide to dance in the first place, you ask? Simple: so that I could support myself while I was in school. I needed a job that could work around my full-time schedule as a student, and I didn't want to break my back making coffee for minimum wage. I knew girls that danced to save money: to travel, for tuition, to start a business. I didn't save—I danced to pay the bills.

What can I say about being a Native girl working in an industry that "objectifies" women? If you've got your head screwed on straight, you'll survive; if you don't, you'll become a statistic. It takes a certain type of individual to dance. Some girls get forced into it. Some girls choose it. Not all girls get the opportunity to dance. You have to possess the three Bs: beauty, brains and balls.

It's unfair, but I fit the stereotype of the "Indian princess," whether I like it or not: a soft voice, light complexion, dark chokecherry eyes and a body like a racehorse. Some girls use cheesy gimmicks like dressing up as a nurse or a French maid, but it never crossed my mind to use my heritage as a "selling point." I couldn't see myself coming out on stage dressed in a long feather war bonnet and a buckskin bikini accessorized with black-light war paint, while the dj announced my entrance: "Fellas, put your hands together for . . . Dances for Dollars! This wild, untamed beauty is the last of her tribe . . ."

Every once in a while some non-Aboriginal patron would have a little story about a "Native girl I once knew," which would be nothing more than a glorified tale about how she could drink like a fish or fight like a man or get irately jealous over another girl.

I've always been curious about the psychology associated with stripping. Let me tell you—you really find out what people are made of when they learn you're a stripper. One particular situation will always stay with me. Helen,* the overly concerned principal of the institution I was studying at, pulled me out of class for a "meeting" in her office. The air in the room felt thick with urgency, and the stress settled into my muscles, because in my experience, nothing good ever came out of a visit to the principal's office. Then, before she'd said a word, Helen handed me an article about the missing Vancouver women whose remains had ended up in the yard of a pig farm. At that moment I knew precisely what she was getting at: she had taken it upon herself to "save" me from the downward spiral I was about to descend, called stripping.

I was very apprehensive about the direction this meeting was going. I could understand Helen's concern about exploitation and being a Native woman and yada yada yada. But what really made my skin crawl was the fact that this woman, whom I had just met at the beginning of the school year, suddenly told me she loved me: "I'm saying this to you because . . . I love you." She was making unblinking eye contact with me when she said this, and there wasn't another person around. You can imagine how uncomfortable this made me, being told "I love you" by an older woman in a position of authority. I thought that she was gonna kiss me or something, and that scared the hell out of me, because I'm not gay (not that there's anything wrong with that).

---

* The names of people in this essay have been changed.

That really messed with my head. Being told those three little words by anyone other than your family is a little frightening, whether you want to hear them or not. I couldn't help it—my first reaction was shock, and then I burst into tears. I hadn't seen my family or friends for six months and must have been awfully lonely, so hearing those words pierced my tough-girl exterior. In hindsight, the whole situation angers me because Helen tried to manipulate me into quitting my job. A job she didn't know anything about, a job that requires one to be strong, not weak.

As I sat there sniffling like a little bitch, Helen tried to "identify" with me by sharing her own fucked-up past. Unfortunately the story was an all-to-common one for Native women: coming from a broken home and wanting to escape the poverty, moving to the city as a teenager to realize her dreams, only to hook up with the wrong guy, a drug dealer. Do you see where this is going? So basically she ended up in the bell jar for a number of years: "We smoked more hash than we sold."

But Helen didn't know the first thing about me. All she knew was that I was a girl from Saskatchewan who wanted to study theatre. What she didn't know was that I didn't lack intelligence or common sense and that I had actually put a lot of thought into my after-school job. I had done my research, and my boyfriend at the time, Matt,* was very supportive.

Matt was my first private dance. We planned it out. When I was finished my first stage dance, I got dressed and looked for him in the crowd. I pretended to be "Marissa," and he pretended to be someone else. I was so nervous, and—oddly enough—so was he.

My motto used to be *Good girls are the bad girls who don't get caught*, but that all changed one night when my friend and mentor walked into the club. The strip club is a nexus in society that connects people who wouldn't normally meet, but on this slow Monday in the VIP lounge, it brought me face to face with someone I knew, not to mention respected and admired.

Up until that night, I had only ever told two other adults about how I subsidized my student income. They were the general manager and artistic director of the theatre company I used to work at before I moved to Toronto, and we were eating brunch in the restaurant of the hotel they were staying at. They looked at me as if I were crazy. "What if one night you're on stage and a big group of chiefs walks in and sits down right in front of the stage while you're dancing?" they asked. "I guess they would be tipping me with their travel per diems," I joked. I had never thought about bumping into anyone I knew, since I was living three thousand kilometres from home.

Well, it didn't happen with the big delegation of chiefs—it was just one blue-eyed Ojibway that made my world collide with reality. I saw him sitting at the bar, and I was pretty sure he'd seen me. I didn't want to be rude, especially if he had seen me, so I made my way over.

"Hey you," I said, trying to balance the real me with my stripper persona.

"Oh my God!" He looked just as busted as I felt. "Well if it ain't Simone from Saskatchewan! How are you doing?" My cover was blown, even though it was just the bartender and a few patrons within earshot. As far as I was concerned, I was savvy Malaysian Marissa, not naive Simone from Saskatchewan. I had to decide whether to be Marissa or me. I picked Marissa, but the real me, that awkward girl, kept slipping in. I knew he felt a little weird too, but the wine he was drinking had loosened him up. I wondered if there was a chance I could entertain him with a dance or two; I had to slip in my pitch. We made small talk, then I asked the question that was looming over us.

"So . . . do ya wanna?" I looked over at the private dancing booths that lined the walls, individually shrouded by thick velvet curtains.

The reality of the situation hit him. "Uh . . . don't take this the wrong way, you're beautiful, but . . ."

I already knew the answer, and it wasn't yes.

I used my fake plastic smile. "Hey, that's okay. Maybe another time. It was nice talking to you."

I knew that was the last time I would be asking anyone for a dance. I left the VIP lounge and took the spiral staircase up to the dressing room. I didn't pack up my locker. I left all my outfits: the schoolgirl, the starlet and the vixen. And my dancing licence.

That was my last night as a stripper.

YOU CAN ALWAYS
COUNT ON AN
ANTHROPOLOGIST

(To Set You Straight, Crooked
or Somewhere In-between)

Gregory Scofield

ESTERDAY I SPENT the better part of the afternoon
thumbing through the *Alberta Elders' Cree Dictionary*,
hoping to find a word or description for "two-spirited," a
label remotely close to its English counterpart, like homosexual,
queer, transsexual, transvestite . . . But the closest I could come
to such a word was *nîso achâhkowak*, which literally translates to
"two spirits" and which if used in a sentence might read, "The
house was haunted by two spirits."

Apparently the Cree elders were as mystified as I was about
the whole two-spirited description. How do you translate such a
concept, the idea of a third or fourth gender? After all, don't we
carry the spirits of our mother and our father, our grandmoth-
ers and our grandfathers? Moreover, on a purely biological level,
our gender appears to be determined by the X or Y chromosome.
Then again, who really knows what sacred ceremony takes

place inside the womb? To my mind, the Cree dictionary is also deplete of the word "hermaphrodite."

Nevertheless, the afternoon wasn't entirely wasted. I stood at the kitchen window watching the late October leaves fall in tufts of two or three, reciting the new words I'd learned: *ka nîsohkwakanehk*, two-faced; *nîswayak kohpakarnahikehk*, two-fisted; *nîswaw*, twofold; *nîspîwâpiskos*, two pence; *nîswaw ka pimastek*, two-ply. But I found myself chanting the word *nîskwayak ka itapatahk* over and over. The image of my late aunty suddenly came to mind. I could see her watching the kitchen clock, her eyes dark and stormy. "*Wahk-wa*, Harry!" I could hear her say. "*Tapway ê-kimôcitan!* Dat sneaky doo-diming son of a bitch husband of mine!"

If Harry was a doo-dimer, I began to think, then was he also two-spirited? Did he possess a good husband spirit and a bad husband spirit? Did those spirits ever come into conflict, ever come to blows? And was Harry the bingo-playing version of Sybil, the famous schizophrenic whose multiple personalities stumped everyone from psychics to psychiatrists? *Nîskwayak ka itapatahk*—I wondered, are we all genetically built to be doo-dimers? And if so, does this mean we're all two-spirited?

But this wasn't the first or second time I had pondered the politics of identity. In fact, most of my writing career has been punctuated by labels such as "angry," "streetwise," "Métis," "gay" and "two-spirited." It seemed with each new book I was helped into yet another coat of identity, and although there was a certain truth to each one, I found the coats of academics or reviewers, even other Native people, ill-fitting or too restrictive. Yet I understand the wearing of coats and colours, badges and buttons. Perhaps even the "two-spirited" badge, the term itself, had been coined by gay American Indians. Having worked with gay, lesbian and transgendered Native people, I fully understood the need for solidarity and a sense of uniqueness, a defined

and supportive place among the dominant white gay male culture. Racism, class discrimination and sexism can be even worse
within our own community than they are in general society. Furthermore, the daily burdens of family and ostracism carried by
many urban gay/lesbian/transgendered Native people only add
to their sense of isolation and disconnection.

I hadn't heard the term "two-spirit" until the late '80s. On
my own quest for sexual/cultural understanding and acceptance,
I searched out books on the topic. There were two particular
books that I found insightful: *The Spirit and the Flesh: Sexual
Diversity in American Indian Culture* by Walter L. Williams (Bea-
con Press, 1986, 1992) and *The Zuni Man-Woman* by Will
Roscoe (University of New Mexico Press, 1991). Both books
are anthropological in scope, espousing the idea of sacredness
among those individuals born with both male and female spirits.
Both authors elaborated on the cultural and spiritual significance of such individuals, citing the Zuni world view of multiple
genders and the bestowing of holy powers. This embodiment
of multiple genders greatly intrigued me, although I found it
difficult to understand in relation to the Cree spiritual world and
the teachings I'd been taught. One's sacredness or *pawatew*, the
spirit helper who becomes part of one's identity, defines one's
lifelong responsibilities, and one's lifelong responsibilities define
one's sacredness, one's *pawatew*.

Nonetheless, this confusing but politically fringed coat
remains hanging in my closet. I grew up in a household of women
where the teapot sat on the table, a piping hot goddess whose stories were steeped in Métis and *nehiyawewin*, Cree traditions. I
grew up with lace that warmed winter windows and the smell of
Pine-Sol, smoked moosehide and cinnamoned apples. I grew up
learning to cook and sew. I grew up learning the finer qualities
of intimacy and diplomacy. I learned to pee sitting down. And
I learned to deaden myself to my stepfather's rages, to gather up

my mother's bones after one of his beatings. And always the teapot, our goddess, was ready to speak of wars both won and lost.
I grew up among warrior women, hearing their songs of sister-
hood and survival. I grew up singing beside them, and I carry
their songs to this day.

And yet my sense of masculinity, my own state of being
male in the world, suffered a great deal. My fear of men was
largely influenced by my mother and my aunties, an uneasy co-
habitation of tyrant and loyalist, perpetrator and protector. It
seemed appropriate to blame my vacant father, my abusive stepfather and uncle for all of our suffering. Men, or so I believed,
were the epitome of everything wrong in the world. They could
neither demonstrate love nor compassion, understanding nor
acceptance. To complicate matters even more, my adolescent
attraction towards men made me feel ashamed and disloyal. My
body felt like a liability, my desires a muddled dichotomy of lust
and loathing. The very thought of surrendering myself emotionally, mentally, spiritually or physically to another man filled me
with panic. I vowed not to repeat the mistakes my mother and
aunties had made. Instead, I was able to detach my body from my
mind. I learned to use sex as a self-indulgent weapon. Little did I
know that the majority of the human race had learned the exact
same. This revelation, however, was my first real insight into
men. They, too, could be vulnerable and suspicious, sacred and
filled with self-doubt. They, too, were capable of feeling emotion, although I now realize society does not, for the most part,
support this notion. Over time my own sense of masculinity was
also shaped by these expectations. So perhaps, given my childhood, I was fortunate to be raised by women, to develop my own
idea of masculinity and its meanings.

But still one's sacredness, one's *pawatew*, like sexual identity
itself, is not easy to define. I've often wondered if the act of sex
or the refusal of it between lovers can be considered two-headed,

two-hearted, two-spirited? Or is the act of sex simply just that—
an act? An acting out of love and hate, tenderness and brutality,
joy and sorrow, freedom and captivity; an unconscious demon-
stration of our two-headed, two-hearted, two-spirited selves? Or
does it simply come down to the mysterious site of our bones and
our quest to uncover their ancient meanings, our own anthropological dig into self and spirit? Moreover, when we brush
away the dirt of societal expectations, do we find our bones in a
state of straightness or crookedness or somewhere comfortably
in between? And who among us, having experienced love and
hatred, tenderness and brutality, joy and sorrow, freedom and
captivity, can say that there is only one way to excavate our true
sacredness, our *pawatew*?

These thoughts lead me back to the teapot from my childhood, the goddess whose stories were steeped in *nehiyaw*, Cree
tradition, and whose stories flowed, piping hot, filling my imagination. My aunty Georgina's stories about the northern lights,
love medicine or Wihtikiw, the Legendary Eater of Humans,
were veiled in mystery, complicated like the brightly coloured
beads she stitched into place on a pair of moccasins. These were
nighttime stories—stories that she'd picked from the muskeg,
stripped from the birch trees, lifted from beneath a rock and
placed upon the table, beside the tin of bannock and the teapot.
These were stories not meant for TV or books. These were stories
that could not be recorded, stories that had to be held and passed
around like a newborn baby. These were stories meant to teach a
small boy how to use his strength and senses, his awareness and
instinct. These were lifetime stories, gifts of *maskihkîy*, medicine.

This type of "thought" medicine, I believe, can be brewed
from the most seemingly insignificant root. My bookshelf, for
example, has become a sacred lodge of poetic singers, young and
old storykeepers, trickster-talkers, political warriors and history
weavers. Whereas once I only housed the books of Aboriginal

authors, I've learned to open my lodge to anyone who thinks in terms of medicine and the passing of sacred knowledge—anyone who wishes to add his or her gift to the giveaway ceremony of communal stories.

One such story came to my attention many years ago. It was the collected work of a white anthropologist who'd spent years among the Plains Cree on the Little Pine reserve in Saskatchewan, documenting the traditions and customs of the people who lived there. At first I was not interested in yet another anthropological dig into the Native psyche. A few moments later, however, I was drawn back to the book. It was the work of a white anthropologist, I reasoned, and therefore I was entitled to edit his research for inaccuracy, for gross misinterpretation. I flipped through the index and was astonished by the pages of information. Everything I wanted to know about Cree kinship terms, male and female roles, the raising of children, storytelling and mythical beings, art and games, birth and death, housing and food preparation, social customs and vision quests, was at my fingertips.

I followed the long column of words beginning with the letter H until I found the word *homosexuality*. According to the anthropologist and his Cree informant, named Fine-Day, there was a gay precursor before me, the Cree version of the Lakota *winkte*; the Mohave *alyhas*; the Navajo *nadle*; the Zuni *Ihamana*; the Tewa Pueblos *quetho*; the Crow *bade*; the Cheyenne *he man eh*; the Omaha *mexoga*; the Zapotec *ira' muxe* and the Aleut *shopan*.

My Cree forerunner was called *ayekkwew*, "neither man nor woman" or "man and woman." It was reported that Piciwiskwew, which was said to mean "he moves and makes his home/house among women," died from wearing a dress that had been worn by a menstruating woman. He had been killed by the power of the woman's menstrual blood just as the Cree believed a man would have been. Only if he had been born a woman would he not have been harmed.

I was alarmed by the story, and yet at the same time I was intrigued by the phenomenon, the spiritual significance of Piciw-iskwew's death. This was, or so it appeared, brought about by his born gender and his male inability to nullify the spiritual/physical power of women. I couldn't help but wonder, would wearing a dress that he made himself have protected him? Furthermore, I recall thinking seriously about the idea of two-spiritedness. If the Creator had gifted Piciw-iskwew with two-spirits, then why had his female power not protected him? Moreover, if Piciw-iskwew knew the consequence of wearing the menstruating woman's dress, then why had he done so?

Although the story was difficult to understand, I did come to a certain conclusion. Piciw-iskwew's death was a direct result of him breaking Cree spiritual law. The female energy and his male physical being had in the end killed him. Did this mean, therefore, that the idea of two-spiritedness among the Cree was conceptual rather than spiritual?

As I mentioned earlier, I was raised exclusively by women. The homes/houses of my childhood were far removed, at least emotionally, from the homes/houses of men. Had you known my women, the indignity they suffered, you would not blame them. I have only recently, in my own home, learned to live among men comfortably. My *niwicewakan*, "the one I go around with," is loving and kind. He is the son of a farmer, smart in the ways of landscape and animals. His father has the sight to predict bad weather and strange happenings, although he does not believe in omens. He often teases me about my taste for wild meat but never complains about my cooking. He once told me that I was a hard worker, a good housekeeper. He thanked me for hemming his pants. I took the compliment, giving thanks to my *iskwewak*, my women.

So does this make me two-spirited in my father-in-law's eyes? I'm certain if I asked him, he would look at me strangely as if I had said, "Do I look like a farmer today?" Knowing him as I do, his response would go something like this: "Jesus Christ— you're a human being like everyone else!" A human being, yes. And like all human beings, I strive to understand my *pawatew*, my lifelong responsibilities. The lessons and teachings I've received from both men and women.

Based upon the anthropologist's interpretation and spelling of the word *ayekkwew*, I found nothing close to its meaning in the Cree dictionary. I did find, however, two similar words: ayak- kwemaw *pl.* ayakwemawak (VTA): *The words spoken give her/him a tough time*, i.e.: *it is a reprimand*. I also found the word ayah- kweyihtamowin *pl.* ayahkweyihtamowina (NI): *Being diligent; diligence*. My best (and not so fluent) interpretation of these words as they relate to two-spiritedness is: *It may constitute a tough time hearing strong words, but be diligent.*

My own diligence, both steady and wavering, to understand and accept my Creator-made self, my God-given power, my *pawatew*, is still steeping in my spirit. Until I fully understand the gifts I've been given, I'm grateful for the sight of my two eyes, the ability to create with my two hands. So again, does this make me two-spirited? Perhaps. Perhaps not. I do know, however, that Turtle Island is a place of sacred and not so sacred people, all of us looking for a sense of belonging, a validation of our existence— maybe even a platform to stage our resistance, for whatever reason. One could conclude, I suppose, that these inherent needs are one and the same, an endless step towards self-definition. Then again, perhaps definition is really about interpretation.

Take the simple act of eating together. Many potatoes ago, I sat down for dinner with my adopted Cree brother and his fam- ily. Quite casually, I asked him, *"Peta een patakwa."* He looked up from his plate disapprovingly, as if I'd asked him to pass the kitchen stove. "We don't say *een patakwa*," he corrected. "That's what half-breeds call them. The proper way to say it is *n-patakwa*."

He slid the bowl of potatoes across the table, digging back into his proper spuds. A few moments passed uncomfortably. Being a half-breed myself, half devil/half angel, as my aunty used to say, I mentally slipped off to my own secretive coulee. The potato resistance of 1982 was about to begin.

"Hey bro," I said, "if I'm gonna eat my *n-patakwa*, I'll need you to pass me a *mistemihkwan*." My sister-in-law dropped her face, trying desperately to quell her laughter.

Even the half-breeds knew an *etimihkwan* was not dinner conversation. A spoon, which in Cree has a double (female) meaning for . . .

And to think I'd made inference to my bro being not just any old spoon. But a big spoon. A huge, self-important spoon that could dish up more *een patakwa* than a forklift. At that, he left the table. Within seconds, the resistance was over. And Riel and Dumont both enjoyed a good smoke.

FIRST WIVES CLUB

Salish Style

Lee Maracle

---

*T*HERE IS AN old saying: "The older you get, the less sex you have, and the more you talk about it." If you'll pardon the pun, that makes older people oral experts on sex when it is a little late to be considered sexy . . . This society is focused on projecting sexiness only through youth, but many of our elders don't buy into that idea much, and of course neither do I. Falling in love and being sexy are not always tied together, but falling in love inspires us all to fall back on the sexy machinations of our youth. As long as sexual desire burns inside we remain sexy and thus forever young. I had an opportunity to witness one of my elders fall in love in her sixties, and it struck me how much romance became her. Sexy seems to have more to do with desire and aliveness than anything else.

Every now and then my son phones me to tell me he is reading some article or other about sex, which is a good thing for a young Salish man to be doing, as you will see later on from the story. He called me some time back to say that sex burns calories and, if the scientists he was quoting were correct, it burns them up at the rate of 3,500 calories a romp. He added that sex was also purported to clear the skin of unsightly blemishes and to help clear the mind. All of which made me wonder why more of us don't just give up our treadmills, track shoes, skin potions and brain vitamins and opt for a daily romp. On another occasion my son called to tell me that sex is a powerful source of energy and, better still, a source of energy that can only be replenished by consuming it. I replied, "Too bad." "Too bad," he asked? "Yeah," I answered, "I just can't picture anyone giving an engineer permission to figure out a way to harness the energy, which is too bad . . . , such a waste."

Despite all of the above, my son says that he heard that the average person in Canada (and I'm not quite sure how this estimate was arrived at) only has sex once a week. I imagine Canadians using billions of tonnes of skin products annually to little avail and then swallowing a bunch of vitamins before they run off to public and private gyms, spas, fat farms, etc., which are becoming more numerous year to year as the baby boomers acquire that old middle-age spread and sigh. Makes you wonder.

First Nations people, particularly 55+ women, are not billed as sexy anywhere by anyone; generally, coupling (pardon the pun) First Nations women with sex is done crudely when it is done at all. There are no First Nations supermodels or sexual icons out there, so procreative sex is spoken about without fanfare and with a certain measure of disregard for the femininity and the beauty of the women being referenced. Don Burnstick is a comic who looks funny and makes funny faces, so when he says "I saw a beautiful Ojibway woman once" and makes a face, people laugh. When he follows it with, "It could happen," only half the audience laughs, because for some of us this "joke" is not all that fun or funny. Underlying his sense of humour is the disqualification of the sexiness of an entire nation of women. Salish humorists try very hard to poke fun at human folly without completely disqualifying humanity itself. We try to have fun with each other and not at each other's expense.

Western society's values have always confused me. On the one hand, sexiness in young women is desired, but on the other hand, for a very long time the sexy woman engaging in sex was considered immoral.

"What good does it do to cajole and persuade a woman into having sex with you, then humiliate and berate her for it when she gives in?" this old chief asked some white guy a couple of hundred years ago. It seems that while women are burdened with the responsibility of being sexy, permission to engage in sex is generally considered a male prerogative, although that attitude is changing slowly. Men have come a long way, baby, in the sexual department (again, pardon the pun). This shift is good for me: as I age, the burden of carrying a bad reputation weighs and fatigues.

So what is sexy? I have to say that the act itself seems hilarious to me, when I am not engaged in it. There is nothing we do that is so much fun but looks so ridiculous as when two people fumble around, roll around and then bounce up and down on each other, all the while uttering odd grunts and sighs. The prelude to sexual intercourse, though, is lovely. When sexual desire is sparked up no matter how old we are, our movements become elegant and smooth, determined, nearly urgent and sure, and our voices acquire that husky come-hither musicality that is so sweet. We feel our curves; our chests/breasts push themselves out almost with a will of their own. Our hips sway, and our nipples perk up and become sensitive. We can feel the desire rising from our loins. Our skin tingles. Whatever stresses and worries we have on our minds slip away for the moment. We lean into the conversation of a prospective lover, soften our voices, twirl our fingers in our hair and bat our eyes. We giggle and laugh at jokes we wouldn't normally consider funny. We reach out and sneak secret little touches, extend quick and secretive caresses in those forbidden places, move into our significant other, brushing nipples against his arm or his chest in feigned innocence, as though it were an accident. We imbibe the world around us with sexual meaning, which gives birth to some good old sexually laden double entendre:

"Coffee?" he purrs side-glancing, eyes intense with desire and full of some crazy kind of knowing where this is leading.

"Oh, yeah," I answer, lips swelling, thighs quivering; my mouth relaxes and pouts. I am careful not to completely close it. I am doubly careful to hold the pout. My tongue plays an old game of sneak up with my barely open mouth. He looks at me with lascivious intent, sucks wind and holds. Oh yeah, this is going where I want it to.

"Sugar?" He drawls as though he considered it my very essence, my name.

"Yesss . . ." I am very near to orgasm. Yup, this is where I want to be.

In the modern world men are expected to court women, but in the Salish world, this transformation is in its infancy. In the original Salish cultures, it was the women who chose the partners, and our women elders negotiated the marriage, *if* there was going to be one. If a woman desired a man and no marriage was in the offing for her, she was going to have an affair of the heart, because for sure, women were free to indulge in sexual activity when and if they pleased. Unlike in some other First Nation cultures, sex and morality were not that tightly connected (again, pardon the pun).

As a young person my chiefs asked me to organize the youth and encourage them to attend the first all chiefs' conference in Kamloops, B.C. So I called a youth gathering to be held at the local Indian Friendship Centre in Vancouver, notified all the young people I knew and made a presentation on behalf of the not-quite-fully-formed Union of B.C. Indian Chiefs. It was 1968, the year the skimpy, sexy T-shirt came on the scene for young women. I was wearing one. Along with my skimpy T-shirt I had on a pretty snug pair of jeans and no bra (it *was* the sixties). An elder from Saskatchewan named Ernest Tatoosis came up after my talk and complimented my speech. After a pregnant pause he added, staring at my cleavage (small though it was), "But maybe you should dress more traditional," and he pointed at my shirt. I knew what he meant. He was well known for scolding women for wearing sexy clothing. "Real Indian women wore dresses, long dresses, covering their legs and buttoned to the neck." I suddenly remembered a picture of a group of First Nations men dressed in Western pants, shirts and sporting little mini-skirts and holding old rifles. Should I tell him that I will wear a long dress buttoned to the neck if he wears that mini-skirt? He probably wouldn't get it. "You're right," I answered instead, and I removed my shirt.

Cree women apparently wore long dresses (deerskin) before Europeans arrived and traditionally covered their bodies pretty much head to toe. What Tatoosis did not know was that, prior to the arrival of the good Oblates, Salish women did not wear shirts during the summer or at a good old bone game.

In this era of Aboriginal Studies, there is a tendency to red-wash or clean up our past before passing on our traditions, and sometimes it gets cleaned up in accordance with someone else's current morality. I am not advocating a return to the old lahal games practices, in which women sang and danced half-naked, enthusiastically cupping and bouncing their beautiful breasts in an attempt to distract the other team, but we should know a little about who we are before we become someone else's idea of who we should be. Sex, whether it is hetero- or homosexual, is so central to adult human interaction—every adult at some point feels their loins fire up with desire, and sexiness is our response to it.

Sexual permission, however, is structured by the social milieu from which we arise.

One time, a fellow wolf clan woman from the Six Nations told me she was going to visit my home. She is like many Six Nations women—sexy, tall and with one of those lyrical, husky and luscious voices we all love to listen to.

"So, you are going to have fun with the little people," I said, adding that we were the "cutest people in the world."

She did. She returned and said that everyone there was short and thin and, exactly like I'd said, cute. Even the men, she added with a delicious laugh. She said they were so cute and so small, she wanted to put a couple of them in her coat pocket and take them home.

"The men would just come up to me and look at me smiling. It was so funny, so odd. What was that all about?"

"They were making a pass," I said. "The smile is telling you, 'I'm available and willing.'"

"You mean all I had to do was grab one of them and take him home?"

"Pretty much," I said.

"No wonder West Coast women are so aggressive," she laughed.

Which brings me to the story and the teachings I acquired before my body opened itself up to sexual desire.

Our stories are told in sections. This section teaches women to use "weasel medicine" to manipulate men to do the right thing by their families. It also teaches us about the power of women, their desire and their sexiness, and it grants women permission to engage their sexuality in a way that they see fit.

It was after the flood; the tide waters were receding. The earth had cleaned up much of the cadaverous mess that had been left over after the loss of so much mammalian life. Our response to the flood was not as tidy as the Christian one. First, God did not pay us a visit to warn us beforehand that it was coming, although the Creator visited some of us to tell us where to find safe places while we were thrashing about in the midst of the tsunami that occurred. This story might have turned out different if God had given us either the time or instructions to build an ark and climb aboard with all the paired animals.

When the flood hit us, most of us perished. The only women that survived were the ones who had made it to the tops of some very large mountains with help from one sister or another. The heroes in most of our flood stories are women—sisters who saved elders, other sisters, their children or sacrificed themselves for expectant mothers and the like. The women did not generally rescue men; at least if a woman did rescue a man, the story did not get handed down in my family. My mother and grandmother used to say that women did not try to save the men because they couldn't save both men and women, and although it takes all the women to repopulate the village, it takes only one man.

One such pair of sisters, one of whom had rescued the other, climbed down from the mountain on which they had waited out the flood as the waters receded. They were determined to make a go of it on the valley floor at the ocean's edge below. They constructed a lean-to from cedar woven mats and began life anew. One day, one of the women was at the river's mouth, where the ocean meets the shore, and she was washing out the mats when she spotted a canoe. It wasn't a big canoe. Inside it was a solitary man. There he was, standing in the canoe looking towards her. Behind him the sun dappled diamond glints of light as it fell behind the sea, reddening the sky and silhouetting his perfect body. Her legs quivered, and her lips swelled. Oh yes, he was yummy, so pretty he hurt to look at.

She decided she would have him. Now, Salish women know how to capture a man. She turned her back on him and began singing an old love song. She leaned forward, her butt sticking out, and rotated her hips, swaying them to the music of her song. Salish women know that Salish men love that little bumblebee dance of the hips. Sure enough, the man paddled ashore. As he arrived, she turned her face towards him slightly, just enough so that he could see the fire of desire in her eyes, but she kept singing and swaying and of course washing her mats. Humans are funny. We don't want to seem too obvious, so we pretend to be doing something, anything, but seducing the person we are seducing, while we leer, we poke out our butts and our breasts, bat our eyes and just generally do anything we can to get laid.

He landed, tied up his canoe and followed her to her lean-to. They got busy. He stayed all winter, and she became pregnant. The woman already had a child, and this child nagged the man. He became increasingly annoyed, and as he became annoyed he grew restless for the sea. Spring rolled around, and so he hopped into his canoe and hit the sea waves. After he left both joy and tragedy struck the sisters. They ran out of food. Because one of them was pregnant the other gave up her food for her sister and her child, and soon she died. The woman left standing knew that the loss of her sister meant the loss of her sister's assistance, and the winter became increasingly difficult and fraught with hardship. Still, she and the children survived.

The weather began to change in the fall, and the man returned. She was digging for clams and saw him approach. Excited and relieved, she started to sing again, turning her back and pushing up those hips he loved so much and swaying back and forth to the rhythm of her song. He parked his canoe. On her back was this baby, but he didn't know what it was. He asked her, "What's that ugly thing on your back?"

"You don't know?" she purred, and she trotted her fingers along his arm, his chest and his face. The purring pull of her husky voice distracted his mind and woke up his other head. She picked up her basket of clams and headed for shore. She moved elegantly, slowly and rhythmically, her hips swaying and the light catching them in a magical way as she waltzed her way through the sun-dappled trail. He followed her, focused on those hips and his own desire. Soon he forgot his question. All summer long he complained about the noisy ugly thing, but she never said anything to him when he did. "Let him complain," she thought—"I know how to quiet him," and she would trail her fingers across his chest and imagine the stories of his journey through the flood for him, telling him how brave and strong he was in her husky come-hither voice. When she did his mouth dried, his legs quivered and invariably he would end up in her lean-to, forgetting about his complaints. Eventually he would grow restless. As he was getting ready to leave that next spring, he pointed to the baby and asked her again, "Where did you get that thing?"

"You don't know?" she answered.

"No," he said.

"You will know when you need to know," she answered coyly, then lifted her lashes and turned her face partially towards him in that shy way that excited him. This flustered him a little, as she knew it would, and again he forgot what he had asked. He retreated to his canoe still watching her doing that little bumblebee dance with her hips as she swayed through the trail, the sunlight bouncing first off this hip, then off the other hip. It excited him so to watch her make her way back to her lean-to. He wasn't sure he wanted to leave. He left only after deciding he would always return. She smiled to herself, took one last glance and murmured to herself, "he's coming back for more."

He had spent all summer at her camp. While he was there she had him fix her up an adze and clear the old dead logs that littered the small delta prairie. When he was done she had him split shakes from the short thick cedar logs and shave the thinner long ones free of their bark. She was making plans for his return.

In the fall he returned just a little earlier this time than before. In fact, summer was barely over when he came back. Again she had another child on her back. Again he asked her where she got that ugly thing and again and again she lifted her lashes, traced her fingers along his arms and pressed her breasts against his chest and asked if he wasn't just a little tired. "I'm not that tired," he answered with more enthusiasm than he intended. As she pressed her leg up against him she could feel the swell of his manhood. The question receded.

He worked with even more vigour this time clearing the delta of old dead wood and making tools for her. She had built a weir from the thin long trees he had cut for her the last time he spent the summer. After he had skinned them and left, she staked the river and trapped a lot of fish. Now she was busy smoking them. She offered him a bite. It was tasty. The food was getting better, the young man thought, and he noticed that the food was much more plentiful than the first time he had come. He was less inclined to wander, but the first baby was now walking and often had a snotty nose, which annoyed him. The little thing was demanding much of her time and eventually he grew impatient and again he became determined to leave, although this time it was early winter by the time he dragged himself away.

Other women who survived the flood saw the smoke of the woman's fire and noticed that the clearing had increased in size. They decided to leave the mountaintops and see how this woman managed to clear so much land so quickly. She invited them to join her and her children. Together they realized they could create a village of survivors. One of the newcomers had a child, so the first woman's children now had a playmate. It was good to have so much company, but the lean-to was not sufficient to protect so many women from the rain. They did their best to build a bigger lean-to, but it was still pretty crowded, and the rain fell cold and damp and the wind chilled them mercilessly.

In the group several young women were without children, and they mentioned this to the woman who was very obviously pregnant again.

"How did you manage to get pregnant?" one asked. "There doesn't seem to be any man around."

"I have a man," she said slyly. "He is off wandering, but he'll be back." And she dipped her hips and let out a sexy growl. They laughed.

"How does that help us?"

"When the weather warms and the tide changes, take the mats to where the ocean meets the river and wash them. If you sing and your behind does that little bumblebee dance, when he comes, he will give you a child." The older women laughed.

"But he is already attached to you. What chance do I have?" one of them sighed.

"Just sing and do that little bumblebee thing, and he won't be able to resist. He doesn't like children, but it doesn't matter because he doesn't know where babies come from," she told them. "Don't tell him."

"Why?"

"The babies annoy him," she replied, and the women found this hugely amusing.

It happened just as the first woman had said. The man came, heard the second woman's song, saw her hips dip and sway and was smitten. Again he saw the first woman with her new child and asked where she got that thing. Again the woman laughed and traced her fingers along his arms, dipped and swung her hips, pressed her breasts against his chest and again he forgot his question. He was smitten with the first woman still. He definitely did not wish to leave. The two women did not mind that he cherished both of them, and they shared his manhood willingly. It was almost too good to be true.

With the man in camp the women were able to go up river and dry their precious shtwehen, gather a wider variety of sweet berries, till the camas fields, dry and smoke clams, gather and dry seaweed and other sea vegetables. As they worked, they sang and danced, told stories of the flood and how they had survived. Their laughter at the antics of their growing children, the attention and industry of the man, all brought joy to the camp. He worked hard, felling trees and splitting shakes for them, but finally the children began talking, nagging him and annoying him, and he still didn't know how these women got them. So early winter he left again. This time all the women gathered at the shore to see him off. As they receded towards the clearing they all sang and swayed their lush hips. The dipping and swaying of all those women pulled and aroused his manhood; the man hesitated, then he saw the children scampering towards the women and he left.

He returned as soon as winter was over. The women were at the edge of the river's mouth. This time they all sang and danced and enticed him to shore. He grew so excited he nearly capsized his canoe. Before they retreated to the lean-to the first woman told him that they needed a home because their lean-to had toppled in a storm; he agreed to build another lean-to. The women gave him a lusty look and purred, "Not a lean-to—a dry and warm home, a big home, a longhouse." As they trailed their fingers along his arms, down his back and across his thighs and pressed their breasts and hips against his chest, his legs, his back, they cajoled him into agreeing to build a longhouse. It didn't take long before he agreed.

As soon as they had his promise they retreated one at a time to the lean-to with him. He managed to satisfy the first two but was exhausted by the time the last woman entered the lean-to. He could not arouse himself. He felt so guilty, but the last woman cooed and whispered, "That's okay—you have good hands and long, thick fingers . . ." He wasn't sure what to do, but the woman seemed to know, and soon she too was satisfied. She wasn't worried; he wasn't going anywhere for a while, and she would have her chance to become pregnant.

He saw the new babies and again asked where they got them. The women giggled, touched his thigh, his chest and his arms, and they all purred, "You don't know?"

To this day no Salish woman has ever broken the promise they made to each other. I know because every time I told my Salish husband I was pregnant he responded with shock: "How did that happen?" And like all good Salish women before me, I just said, "You don't know?" and I traced my fingers along his arms, his chest and his thighs and smiled.

ABOUT THE CONTRIBUTORS

KATERI AKIWENZIE-DAMM is an Anishnaabe writer of mixed blood from the Chippewas of Nawash First Nation. She received an MA in English literature from the University of Ottawa in 1996. She authored *My Heart is a Stray Bullet*, published by Kegedonce Press, and edited *Without Reservation: Indigenous Erotica* and *Skins: Contemporary Indigenous Writing*. She has lived and worked at Neyaashiinigmiing, Cape Croker Reserve on the Saugeen Peninsula in southwestern Ontario since 1994.

JOSEPH BOYDEN is a proud member of the Métis Nation. He is one of eleven children. His first novel, *Three Day Road*, won McNally Robinson's Aboriginal Book of the Year Award, the Rogers Writers' Trust Prize, the Canadian Authors Association Novel of the Year Award, the CBA Libris Fiction Book of the Year Award and was shortlisted for the Governor General's Award for Fiction. It has been published in thirteen languages; a Cree translation, the first ever for a novel, is currently underway.

NANCY COOPER is from the Chippewas of Mnjikaning First Nation. Her work has been published in various anthologies and magazines, and she is currently editing an anthology of indigenous women writing about their fathers and grandfathers. Not one to give up her day job, Nancy works as an adult educator in between bouts of writerly creativity. She lives in Toronto.

MARISSA CRAZYTRAIN (not her real name) is of plains Cree/Saulteaux descent: her great-great-grandmother migrated across the border with Chief Sitting Bull to escape annihilation by the U.S. army and settled in Saskatchewan. "Marissa" no longer dances but waits tables for a more "honest" living. She has turned her experiences of living in Toronto into a one-woman show that premiered at the Saskatoon Fringe Festival.

An Ojibway from the Curve Lake First Nation, **DREW HAYDEN TAYLOR** is widely known for his thoughtful and witty observations on Aboriginal issues. One of Canada's leading playwrights, he has received some of the country's most prestigious drama awards for his work, which includes *Only Drunks and Children Tell the Truth* and the four-part Blues series *The Bootlegger Blues*, *The Baby Blues*, *The Buz'Gem Blues* and *The Berlin Blues*. Taylor also writes for the screen, and his National Film Board of Canada documentary on Aboriginal humour, *Redskins, Tricksters and Puppy Stew*, has been shown across North America and beyond. Currently he is the Writer in Residence at the University of Western Ontario.

Audiences as far afield as France, Germany and Australia have welcomed Hayden Taylor's beguiling storytelling style, and he has given lectures on several continents about Native humour. In 2004 he emceed and performed at an event devoted to the subject at Kennedy Center in Washington, D.C., to celebrate the opening of the Smithsonian Museum of the American

Indian. His trenchant opinions on identity politics and the hilarious absurdities that are often the lot of a "blue-eyed Ojibway" are collected in book form in the *Funny, You Don't Look Like One* series.

TOMSON HIGHWAY is the proud son of legendary caribou hunter and world-championship dogsled racer Joe Highway. Born in a tent pitched in a snowbank, he comes from the extreme northwest corner of Manitoba, where the province meets Saskatchewan and Nunavut. Today, he writes plays, novels and music for a living. Among his best-known works are the plays *The Reẓ Sisters* and *Dry Lips Oughta Move to Kapuskasing* and the bestselling novel *Kiss of the Fur Queen*.

DANIEL HEATH JUSTICE (Cherokee Nation) teaches Aboriginal literatures and Aboriginal Studies at the University of Toronto. He and his partner live with their three dogs in a cabin on the southern shores of Georgian Bay, in the traditional lands of the Huron-Wendat Nation. He is the author of *Our Fire Survives the Storm: A Cherokee Literary History* (University of Minnesota Press), as well as *The Way of Thorn and Thunder*, an indigenous fantasy trilogy published by Kegedonce Press.

MAKKA KLEIST has worked in theatre for the last twenty-seven years as an actor, director, playwright and teacher in Denmark (where she got her education as an actor), Canada, Norway and Greenland. She is now back in her native Greenland, freelancing and working in all aspects of theatre.

LEE MARACLE, Stó:lo Nation, grandmother of seven, mother of four, was born in North Vancouver, B.C., and now resides in Innisfil, Ontario. An award-winning author and teacher, her works include the novels *Ravensong*, *Bobbi Lee* and *Sundogs*; the short story collection *Sojourner's Truth*; the poetry collection *Bent Box*, and the non-fiction work *I Am Woman*. She has co-edited *My Home As I Remember* and *Telling It: Women and Language across Cultures*, edited a number of poetry works and *Gatherings* journals and published in dozens of anthologies in Canada and America. Currently she is Mentor for Aboriginal Students at the University of Toronto, where she is also a teacher, and the Traditional Cultural Director for the Indigenous Theatre School, where she is a part-time cultural instructor.

MICHELLE MCGEOUGH is a member of the Métis Nation of Alberta. Michelle recently completed a Master of Arts degree from Carleton University. Her thesis, *When Two Worlds Collide: Norval Morrisseau and the Erotic*, examines the under-studied area of Morrisseau's erotic body of work. She holds a degree in secondary education from the University of Alberta and a BFA and diploma in Media Studies from the Emily Carr Institute of Art and Design. She is an assistant curator at the Wheelwright Museum of the American Indian in Santa Fe, New Mexico. Michelle is an Institute of American Indian Art alum and an accomplished artist whose work has been exhibited nationally and internationally.

GREGORY SCOFIELD is one of Canada's leading Aboriginal writers whose five collections of poetry have earned him both a national and international audience. He is known for his unique and dynamic reading style that blends oral storytelling, song, spoken word and the Cree language. His maternal ancestry can be traced back to the fur trade and to the Métis community of Kinosota, Manitoba, which was established in 1828 by the Hudson's Bay Company. His paternal ancestry is Jewish, Polish and German—reflective of the experience of immigrants to Canada at the turn of the century. His poetry and memoir, *Thunder through My Veins* (HarperCollins, 1999), is taught at numerous universities and colleges throughout Canada and the U.S., and his work has appeared in many anthologies. He was the subject of a feature-length documentary, *Singing Home the Bones: A Poet Becomes Himself* (The Maystreet Group, 2007) that aired on CHUM TV, BRAVO!, APTN and the Saskatchewan Television Network. He has served as Writer-in-Residence at the University of Manitoba and Memorial University of Newfoundland. He currently lives in Calgary, where he teaches Identity Narratives at the Alberta College of Art & Design.

MARIUS P. TUNGILIK served as Deputy Minister and Regional Director for the Government of the Northwest Territories' Departments of Personnel, Executive and Renewable Resources, and later with the federal public service and the Nunavut Government. He has served on several boards, including the Nunavut Arbitration Board, Nunavut Wildlife Management Board, Inuit Non-Profit Housing Corporation, Safe Shelter, Crisis Line and the Mobile Treatment Program in Nunavut. He lives in Repulse Bay, Nunavut.

DR. NORMAN VORANO is the Curator of Contemporary Inuit Art at the Canadian Museum of Civilization in Ottawa. A graduate of the University of Rochester's Program in Visual and Cultural Studies, his dissertation—*Inuit Art in a* Qallunaat *World: Museums, Modernism and the Public Imaginary, 1949–1962*—examines the promotion, reception and development of Inuit art in North America and Europe. His research interests cover a range of topics in visual culture and art history; he is currently researching contemporary artists from Cape Dorset.